THE OFFICIAL TRAINING MANUAL

MODERN
taekwondo

MODERN
taekwondo

SOON MAN LEE
& GAETANE RICKE

STERLING PUBLISHING CO., INC.

NEW YORK

ACKNOWLEDGMENTS

We would like to thank God for giving us the knowledge, understanding, and ability to make this book possible. We would also like to acknowledge the contributions of Dr. David H. Lasseter, Dr. Ann Brooks, Mr. Robert L. Chapman, Ms. Abrea Torrisi, Mr. J.M. McNeal, and Ms. Lee Etter.

Photos by Henline's Photography

Library of Congress Cataloging-in-Publication Data

Lee, Soon Man.
    Modern taekwondo : the official training manual / Soon Man Lee & Gaetane Ricke.
        p. cm.
    Includes index.
    ISBN 0-8069-3989-3
    1. Tae kwon do. 2. Tae kwon do—Training. I. Ricke, Gaetane. II. Title.
GVGV1114.9.L46   1999
796.815'3—dc20   98–44565
                                CIP

10 9 8 7 6 5 4 3 2 1

Published by Sterling Publishing Company, Inc.
387 Park Avenue South, New York, N.Y. 10016
©1999 by Soon Man Lee & Gaetane Ricke
Distributed in Canada by Sterling Publishing
C/o Canadian Manda Group, One Atlantic Avenue, Suite 105
Toronto, Ontario, Canada M6K 3E7
Distributed in Great Britain and Europe by Cassell PLC
Wellington House, 125 Strand, London WC2R 0BB, England
Distributed in Australia by Capricorn Link (Australia) Pty Ltd.
P.O. Box 6651, Baulkham Hills, Business Centre, NSW 2153, Australia
Manufactured in the United States of America
All rights reserved

Sterling ISBN 0-8069-3989-3

THE WORLD TAEKWONDO FEDERATION

THE WORLD TAEKWONDO FEDERATION
635 YUKSOM-DONG, KANGNAM-KU
TELEPHONE: 82.8.566-2505

SEOUL, KOREA (136)   82.2.557-5448
CABLE ADDRESS: WORLD TAEKWONDO
TELEX: K28870 WTFED FAX: 82.2.553-4728

I take great pride and joy in endorsing *Modern Taekwondo: The Official Training Manual*.

Taekwondo has come a long way from its origins in ancient Korea. A few thousand years ago, Taekwondo was a primitive art. Today, Taekwondo tournaments draw competitors from around the globe. The year 2000 will mark the first time Olympic medals will be awarded for Taekwondo at the Olympic games in Sydney, Australia.

Thanks to the contributions and support of Taekwondo master instructors like Soon Man Lee, Taekwondo has become the fastest growing martial art with the most advanced techniques in the world. Soon Man Lee is well known in the world of Taekwondo for his unmatched knowledge, his teaching, his coaching, and his spreading of the sport in the United States and the international arena.

This book is additional proof of his love and dedication to Taekwondo. His obvious enthusiasm for the sport motivated him in sharing his knowledge with the readers, whether they are beginners or instructors. *Modern Taekwondo* provides an in-depth examination of Taekwondo in all facets—from its international governing body, its rich history, its conditioning exercises, to its many techniques of attacks and defense. I am impressed with the research involved in providing the readers with these factual and detailed information.

As the President of the World Taekwondo Federation, I extend my sincere congratulations to Soon Man Lee and Gaetane Ricke for their efforts in creating this definitive work on Taekwondo. I wish them the best of luck and success with this book.

Dr. Un Yong Kim
Executive Board Member
International Olympic Committee
President, World Taekwondo Federation

THE WORLD TAEKWONDO FEDERATION

THE WORLD TAEKWONDO FEDERATION
635 YUKSOM-DONG, KANGNAM-KU
TELEPHONE: 82.8.566-2505

SEOUL, KOREA (136)   82.2.557-5448
CABLE ADDRESS: WORLD TAEKWONDO
TELEX: K28870 WTFED FAX: 82.2.553-4728

It is with great pleasure that I endorse *Modern Taekwondo: The Official Training Manual.*

I have known Master Soon Man Lee for many years. He has an international reputation for his mastery of the sport. No one understands the pure concepts of the art better than he does. His dedication to the discipline is unmatched by anyone, and his knowledge of all facets of Taekwondo is profound. His enthusiasm for teaching precise techniques has been a guiding force for thousands of his students.

Modern Taekwondo: The Official Training Manual is now the authoritative text for anyone interested in the art of Taekwondo. It is an encyclopedia of the philosophy and history of Taekwondo as well as the many technical aspects of the sport. Master Lee has gone to great lengths to broaden the reader's understanding through photographs and easy-to-follow illustrations.

This book is great for everyone from novices to masters. I strongly recommend it for anyone interested in expanding his knowledge and proficiency of Taekwondo.

Grand Master Chong Woo Lee
Vice President
World Taekwondo Federation

This book is dedicated to the memory of Grand Master Lee's brother, Master Sun Yong Lee (1961–1997). Master Sun Yong Lee was a 7th Dan black belt, a Junior Champion of Taekwondo in Korea, a United States college team coach in 1995, and an international referee from 1989 to 1997.

Preface

Over the years, our Taekwondo students have continually asked us to recommend a good book about the history, art, and practice of modern Taekwondo. Although we feel that there are a few good books on the subject, none satisfy all of the student's needs. In our frustration to locate a truly comprehensive resource, we finally came to one conclusion: write one ourselves.

Modern Taekwondo is the fastest-growing and most advanced martial art form in the world. This book provides a historical perspective of Taekwondo, which is woven throughout the past 2000 years of Korean history. The philosophy of Taekwondo has evolved from its deeply-embedded roots in Eastern religious beliefs and cultures to one that is universally accepted by Taekwondo enthusiasts around the world. The book also describes the role of the World Taekwondo headquarters in the Kukkiwon building in Seoul, Korea, and the World Taekwondo Federation's function as Taekwondo's international governing body.

The technical aspects of the sport are demonstrated in more than nine hundred illustrations and photographs to make it easier to master the sport. The various stances, blocks, self-defense moves, and stylized forms shown in this book help strengthen the body,

sharpen the mind, and build up the spirit for people of all ages. For children, it increases their concentration, builds their self-confidence, and gives them greater self-esteem. It provides teenagers with a proper guidance and solid values. For adults, it promotes good health and adds years to their lives.

Taekwondo is certainly not restricted to those in superb physical condition. As a matter of fact, older students have developed good and powerful techniques. Anyone can take advantage of its benefits when following the proper techniques. Learning is a matter of conviction, not raw physical strength. Regardless of age and gender, Taekwondo is good for everyone.

If you are new to Taekwondo, we recommend that you first check with your physician for any health problems before beginning and, once you know it is safe, then train under the supervision of a qualified instructor who has mastered the various techniques.

Our final bit of advice to learning Taekwondo is to have fun. Fitness without fun is a drudgery, but acquiring the skills of Taekwondo can be a delight for everyone. We appreciate your interest in modern Taekwondo and would like to invite everyone to participate in this art that has tremendous mental and physical benefits.

SOON MAN LEE
GAETANE RICKE

Contents

1

What Is Taekwondo?

Taekwondo is a Korean martial art form that has undergone an autonomous development for more than 2000 years. The word *Taekwondo* literally means the "art of kicking and punching" (*Tae*=foot, *kwon*=fist, *do*=art). It embraces kicking, punching, jumping, blocking, dodging, and parrying. It is a form of self-defense as well as a system of competition whose superior techniques have won it international recognition. From a competitive standpoint, Taekwondo emphasizes power, quickness, and accuracy. Since its techniques are constantly being improved, modern Taekwondo is the fastest growing and most advanced martial art form in the world.

But not only does Taekwondo encompasses physical movements—it is also a system that trains the mind by placing a strong emphasis on the development of moral character and spirit, which are essential for success. As a result, in addition to providing good health and physical fitness, Taekwondo improves concentration, self-confidence, discipline, and patience.

Remarkably, Taekwondo provides a sense of generosity toward those who are weaker. Those who practice the discipline sometimes experience unexpected benefits in their lives, such as a job promotion or better relations with their family, because of the added confidence Taekwondo brings to them.

THE NATURE OF TAEKWONDO

The nature of Taekwondo was derived from two fundamental sets of values obtained from both Chinese and Korean philosophical values. These values, the practical and the ideological, form a proper Taekwondo spirit. Once these two sets of value are combined with the physical activities of the *dojang* (classroom), peace and self-confidence are created among the students.

On a practical value level, you find a personal satisfaction from the physical training. You obtain a sense of accomplishment as you learn the techniques of the art. When you learn self-defense, you feel secure about defending yourself and you gain self-confidence. This practical value is in the elemental movements of each specific technique (either in self-defense, form, or sparring, which all provide physical fitness and good health) and in the principles governing those movements. You will find a balance between two extremes. For instance, when somebody attacks you, you are confident that you can hurt this person but, using your own judgment, you apply only the necessary force to gain control.

The ideological value is an expected behavior from the Taekwondo person based on a set of beliefs from various concepts that cover the entire realm of Eastern philosophy. In this regard, the essence of Taekwondo training is the realization of a relationship between man and nature living in harmony with the universe. This value is found in the three ideals that form the identity of Taekwondo.

The first ideal is technical and based on the practical aspects of training (e.g., being close to nature, achieving meditation through good breathing and fresh air). Taekwondo's practical benefits are bare-handed self-defense and good health through its training. This first ideal is an essential element of Taekwondo training.

The second is the artistic ideal, *Mu Yeh*, which means the art that arises from the union of the mind and soul that is reflected in the action. It is the perfection of movements, beautiful yet powerful, which are achieved through concentration and control. You understand the cooperation between man and nature by getting rid of the ego (the discriminating mind) that controls behavior and using the combination of practice, technique, and concentration. Once the perfection of movement is achieved through this union, you will attain the *Mu Yeh*.

Finally, the third is the philosophical ideal in which theory and actions lead to a good way of life. Its main goal is to convert an introverted mind (controlled by the environment) into an extroverted mind (control of the environment). In other words, through self-confidence and determination, you have a stronger will. Thus, you are able to make positive changes in your life instead of feeling overwhelmed by its problems.

THE TAEKWONDO SPIRIT

A Taekwondo spirit refers to the process of thought in regard to values established through the philosophy and training of Taekwondo. In general, human spirit refers to the wisdom that establishes a way of thinking based on values. Humans, by nature, act and react according to the values that have been set in their minds by their parents, friends, and society.

In the same manner, Taekwondo people respond to the values of the organization. They are respectful and helpful to one another. They do things in moderation and live in harmony. This attitude is established only when you have improved your ability to perceive the relativity of things and act effectively and decisively as a result of training. Once this behavior and a moral philosophy have been established through the assimilation of the Taekwondo ideals (technical, artistic, and philosophical), you have formed a Taekwondo spirit.

This process is both internal and external. The internal process is formed through the absorption of philosophical values from training. During this process, you obtain an active and positive spirit, which commands the universe instead of your being overwhelmed by it. Over time, this process becomes extremely subjective. For this reason, the formation of the spirit might become one-sided or distorted, which means that you might become over-confident or lack some control. At that moment, you need to balance yourself back with the external process or discipline of Taekwondo. The external process is formed through long-term practice as you learn to apply those values into your everyday life. It is important to have the guidance of a qualified instructor, along with the traditional discipline of the *dojang*, plus the practice with a senior partner, to be certain that you are improving in the right direction. This way, you develop the right perception of the value system and moral philosophy that Taekwondo has established through its own history, which helps you to apply it to your own life.

In short, the Taekwondo spirit starts with techniques, develops within the technique, and arrives at perfection through these techniques. Then this Taekwondo spirit is carried throughout your life by applying your value system. The ultimate goal is to mold yourself into a good and balanced human being.

THE PHILOSOPHY OF TAEKWONDO

The philosophy of Taekwondo is the ultimate set of values, originated from Korean philosophy, which is used in Taekwondo to maximize your full potential. These values are of great importance in forming a strong mind and body—the qualities necessary to succeed.

Taekwondo is much more than physical training. It is the formation of a certain character of high moral standards that become a way of living. This process is achieved by first forming a Taekwondo spirit. With this spirit, you find the means to a stable life based upon the harmony between yourself and nature by getting rid of the ego (the discriminating mind) and reaching the *Mu Yeh* (the artistic ideal of the immersion of the soul into the body to achieve perfect action).

The core of Taekwondo philosophy is the concept of duality in nature, which refers to the interaction of opposite forces. When opposite forces are distributed equally, the result is balance, which leads to harmony. For example, if an assailant uses aggressive energy to attack, you should use yielding energy in response. In other words, you should step aside to allow the aggressive energy to flow harmlessly past you. Thus, what was hard (aggressive energy of the attacker) becomes soft (harmless), and what was soft (the yielding energy) becomes hard (the defense against the dangerous assault), allowing balance and harmony to return.

Through Taekwondo training, you can elevate yourself "from mediocrity to excellence." The *Do* in Taekwondo integrates all your training efforts into a unifying energy of the mind and body. You become a whole person through progressive exercise programs that improve concentration and give insight into yourself, which leads to harmony with other people, nature, and the universe.

In short, Taekwondo philosophy teaches you the importance of a healthy body and a sound mind. It creates an awareness of the harmonious interaction of man with his environment when good moral values are followed. Once the student understands this process, he acts and reacts in the best interest of others. He gives only what he would like to receive and accepts only what he would give. The most beautiful aspect of this philosophy is that it benefits everyone regardless of one's religion, personal values, or beliefs.

THE ART VERSUS THE SPORT

Many people think that Taekwondo as an art is different from Taekwondo as a sport. Some believe that Taekwondo is a spiritual art and that the sport side of Taekwondo has no consideration for this. They believe that its only focus is on combat. None of this is true.

If there is a difference between the art and sport of Taekwondo, it is that the art recognizes no rules for combat while the sport of Taekwondo is highly regulated for the safety of its participants. As an art, Taekwondo concentrates on its philosophy, techniques, values, and spirit. But both the art and sport of Taekwondo focus on the technical and mental aspects of the individual to channel one's energy toward a single goal—to live a good and balanced life. Simply put, Taekwondo is Taekwondo. It is an art practiced as a sport. One deals with what is called *Poomse* (form), while the other deals with *Kyorugi* (confrontation). If you are attacked on the street, the rules are suspended and you defend yourself with all the skills you possess. However, when you spar in a controlled environment, you follow stylized forms of blocks, kicks, punches, and other techniques.

Poomse refers to a system of attack and defensive movements done in a set sequence. These basic movements bring together all of the martial art skills in a graceful yet powerful manner. A student develops a certain level of agility as well as breathing control through the movements, which are then fine-tuned through controlled *Kyorugi* with an opponent.

Kyorugi, which was originally used in combat, evolved into a sparring sport with rules and regulations. In the sport there is competition, in the competition there is confrontation, and in the confrontation there is form. The ideal pursuit of the sport is to compete. Although victory is a goal to strive for, it should not be all-consuming.

Both the art and sport have the same values as those of a trusted and virtuous person. Together, they harmoniously exist under the name Taekwondo.

2

History of Taekwondo

Taekwondo's history can be traced back for thousands of years to as far back as 50 B.C. From primitive tribesmen, to feudal soldiers, to contemporary sports enthusiasts, the techniques of Taekwondo have been practiced, refined, and passed on to others. Today, it has evolved into the fastest-growing martial arts form in the world.

Ancestors of modern Koreans settled in tribal states after the neolithic period. They practiced *Tongmaeng*, *Meecho*, and *Kabi*, which were forms of Taekwondo. These forms were later developed into exercises designed to improve physical and mental health.

For several centuries prior to the Christian era, there were battles for control of Korean territories. During this time, Taekwondo underwent some changes and assumed different names. But in spite of this, it still remains the original martial art unique to the Korean culture.

THE THREE KINGDOMS

Three kingdoms ruled parts of the Korean peninsula from 57 B.C. to more than 900 years A.D. The order in which they were established is debated by Korean historians. These kingdoms were loosely organized tribal federations largely controlled by the military who were trained in martial arts that helped develop Taekwondo.

The oldest kingdom was Silla (57 B.C.–A.D. 935), which was founded on the Kyongju plain in southeastern Korea. Silla had a military education and social organization called the *Hwarang* (meaning "Flower Knight"). The young men belonging to the Hwarang were called *Hwarando*, and they were trained in *Tae Kyon* (the original name for Taekwondo). The Hwarang emphasized a strong mind and body, and guided the Hwarando with rigid principles. The Hwarang and the principles they followed were greatly responsible for the unification of the provinces during this period. They helped Taekwondo grow and spread throughout Korea.

The second kingdom was Koguryo (37 B.C.–A.D. 668), which was founded in the Yalu River Valley in the northern part of Korea (Southern Manchuria). Two tombs from this period were discovered—the *Muyong-Chong* and the *Kakjo-Chong*. The walls and ceilings of both tombs are painted with murals depicting the lifestyle of the Koguryo people. One mural of the *Kakjo-Chong* tombs shows two men wrestling. On the ceiling of the *Muyong-Chong* tomb is an illustration of two men fighting in a style similar to Taekwondo.

The third kingdom of Baekche (18 B.C.–A.D.600) was founded in the southwestern part of the Korean peninsula. During the early period, martial arts were discouraged and few records survived. One record that did survive, however, was called *Jae Wang Un Ki*. It indicated the existence of martial art and that it was practiced by common people as well as the military. Their martial arts entailed the use of the hands and feet as in modern Taekwondo.

HWARANDO AND THEIR CODE OF CONDUCT

The roots of the Taekwondo philosophy began during the Silla era when King Jin Heung formed the *Hwarang* organization and introduced the five codes of human conduct. The ideology, which formed the foundation of Korean society, was a combination of the traditional way of life of the tribal communities along with the influence of Buddhism and Confucianism. Buddhist monks often instructed the Hwarang. Won'gwang Popsa, a monk, wrote the five codes of honor on which the Hwarang based its philosophy. These five codes consisted of loyalty to the nation, respect and obedience to parents, faithfulness to one's friends, courage in battle, and avoidance of unnecessary violence and killing. As time went by, more tenets were added to the five codes and eventually the ten commandments of Taekwondo were formed.

THE THREE DYNASTIES

The three dynasties are not to be confused with the three kingdoms. During the three kingdoms, Korea was ruled by kings and emphasis was placed on the division of the boundaries of territories and the specific cultural activities to be adopted. During the three dynasties, the territories were ruled by a succession of rulers from the same family. The emphasis was more on the rules to govern the territories.

During the Silla Dynasty (A.D. 668–935), the Hwarando spread Taekwondo (then called *Tae Kyon*) throughout Korea. It was practiced as a recreation to improve health and fitness.

Ten Commandments of Taekwondo

1. Be loyal to your country.

2. Be a good son or daughter to your parents.

3. Be faithful to your spouse.

4. Be on good terms with your brothers and sisters.

5. Be loyal to your friends.

6. Be respectful to your elders.

7. Respect and trust your teachers.

8. Use good judgment before killing any living thing.

9. Never retreat in battle.

10. Always finish what you start.

During the Koryo Dynasty (A.D. 935–1392), the focus on Taekwondo changed from recreation to combat because of unrest among the civilian population, the military, and the royal household. Its name was also changed from *Tae Kyon* to *Subak*.

Historical records reveal the popularity of Taekwondo during the Koryo Dynasty:

King Uijong admired the excellence of Yi-Ui-Min in Subak and promoted him from Taejong (military rank) to Pyolchang.

The king appeared at the Songchien Pavilion and watched a Subak contest.

The king watched Subak at Hwa-bi Palace.

The king came to Ma-Am and watched a Subak contest.

During this time, King Changjo published *Muye Dobo Tongji*, an illustrated book on martial arts, which included a major chapter on Taekwondo. It said that royalty and persons of high rank have always appreciated Taekwondo. Those who aspired to positions within the military or the royal government were eager to learn Subak, since a significant portion of the tests was devoted to this art.

Taekwondo changed once again during the first part of the Yi Dynasty. Subak became an important national sport, attracting attention from both the royal court and general public. However, in the second part of the Yi Dynasty, its importance declined. Political conflicts and quarrels among the royal family led to an emphasis on education and discouragement of military activities. As a result, Subak remained merely a recreational activity for common people and was diffused throughout the country.

THE 20TH CENTURY

The first half of this century saw great turmoil and transition in Korea. Japanese occupation in 1909 imposed changes on the Korean culture—one of which was the prohibition of practicing martial arts. As a result, masters and students were forced to practice it in secrecy, and their determination actually lead to a revival of Taekwondo. This restriction continued until August 1945 with the declaration of Korean independence.

In 1946, two Taekwondo schools opened in Seoul: *Ji Do Kwan* (also called *Yon Moo Kwan*) and *Chong Do Kwan*. In the city of Gaesung (50 kilometers outside of Seoul), the school of *Song Moo Kwan* was opened. By 1947, the first *Moo Duk Kwan* and *Chang Moo Kwan* schools were opened in Seoul. This process was gradual, since it was during the transition from the Japanese liberation to the Russian influence in their Communist regime.

Prior to the Korean War, Taekwondo masters met to improve their techniques. They shared and combined their personal secrets of martial arts to arrive at a superior form of combat (an important resource in fighting the war). They started with the military first, improving their forms, kicks, and sparring techniques. Tournaments were organized, and they competed among themselves. By the end of 1950, the Korean Taekwondo Association was formed with its main purpose of protecting the quality of the sport. These masters improved Taekwondo to what is known as "Modern Taekwondo."

During the Korean War between the Communist government in North Korea and Republic of Korea in the South, the Russians actively searched for and eliminated famous Taekwondo masters. Among those masters were Grand Master Sang Sup Chon, founder of *Ji Do Kwan*, and Master Pyong In Yoon, founder of *Chang Moo Kwan*. These were great losses to the Korean people. It is believed that, because of this purge, North Korea had no surviving masters until 1972. Many good masters in South Korea were also killed while participating in special commando groups trained in Taekwondo to fight the North.

It is the dream of the Korean people that someday North and South Korea will unify.

In the 1960s, Korean instructors left their country's borders and taught Taekwondo around the world. Taekwondo became known as "Modern Taekwondo" during that decade. Although modern, it was still based upon the *tryung* (patterns) of its ancestral combative arts.

The spread of Taekwondo naturally led to the need for standardized rules and a governing body to enforce those rules. Such an organization was established in May of 1973 when representatives from seventeen nations gathered in Kukkiwon under the guidance of Dr. Un Yong Kim (President of the Korean

Taekwondo Association) to form the World Taekwondo Federation (WTF).

Shortly before the formation of the WTF, Taekwondo had achieved international status when the first World Taekwondo Championships were held in Seoul, Korea. Over the next several years, national organizations and unions were established throughout the world—each of which was guided by the rules established in Kukkiwon.

In 1980, the International Olympics Committee bolstered the popularity of Taekwondo by recognizing the sport during the eighty-third general session. On September 4, 1994, the sport was voted unanimously as an Olympic medal sport for the year 2000.

3
Warm-Up Exercises

In Taekwondo, as in other sports, a warm-up is very important to prepare the body before engaging in vigorous activity. As a martial art, Taekwondo demands physical rigor from its practitioners. All of the body's systems are involved: the heart and lungs as well as muscles and sinew. The joints, hands, and feet are frequently called on to make quick and repetitive strikes. Kicking and punching require tremendous power.

To prevent muscle cramps or other serious injuries to the ligaments and tendons, we strongly recommend that all the warm-up exercises presented in this chapter be performed at the beginning of every practice. We further recommend that warm-up exercises be done with caution. Stretch only to the point of discomfort, not pain. Know your limitations and do not push yourself beyond them. Once the body is warmed up, it should be flexible and then you can proceed with confidence instead of fear of injury.

As you progress in your lessons, you become more flexible and, therefore, more comfortable with the warm-up exercises. Being patient and persistent will be rewarded when you proceed at your own pace.

Knee Bends

With your feet and knees together, bend forward, and place your hands on your knees. Bend your knees as to squat on your heels and return to the original standing position.

Knee Rotation

With your feet and knees together, bend forward, and place your hands on your knees. Move your knees to the right in small circles (eight times). Repeat to the left side (eight times).

Back and Legs

With your hands on your hips, stand straight with your feet shoulder-width apart. Bend forward until your hands touch the floor in front of you. Lift your body up just a little and then go down again, this time bringing your hands behind your legs. Return to your original position and lean as far back as you can. Repeat for a total of eight times.

Waist Bends

Stand with your feet two shoulder-widths apart. Bend forward and twist your upper body by touching your right foot with your left hand. Return to a standing position and then touch your left foot with your right hand. Repeat for a total of eight times.

Inner Thigh and Hip Joints

Sit on the floor with your legs spread apart. Bend forward with your palms extended forward against the floor so that your chin touches the floor. Go as far as you can, then return to an upright position. Repeat for a total of eight times.

WARNING: Do not try this stretch without first getting professional supervision so that you will not strain your thigh muscles and tendons.

Split

Stand straight and slowly slide your right foot forward and your left foot backward until you reach the floor. Stretch forward to touch your right foot with your left hand. Stretch to the other side. Repeat for a total of eight times for each side.

WARNING: Do not try this stretch without first getting professional supervision so that you will not strain your thigh muscles and tendons.

Leg and Back Stretch

Sit with you right leg straight forward and your left leg bent behind you in a hurdle position. Stretch forward and touch your right foot. Return to a sitting position. Repeat for a total of eight times. Switch legs and repeat for a total of eight times.

Thigh and Back Stretch

Sit with your left leg straight forward and right leg bent so that your heel touches your inner thigh. Lean forward and bring your head down to your left leg. Return to a sitting position. Repeat for a total of eight times. Switch legs and repeat for a total of eight times.

Inner Thigh Stretch

Sit down with your heels together close to your body and your hands on your feet. Bring knees up and down so that they flap like a butterfly. Do this for a total of eight times. In the same position, with knees down, bend forward to touch your head to your toes. Go as far as you can reach.

Waist and Hips Stretch

Stand with your feet shoulder-width apart and place your hands on your hips. Rotate the upper body at your hips in a circular motion to the right (eight times). Repeat to the left (eight times).

Side Stretch

Stand with your feet shoulder-width apart and your hands on your hips. Raise your left arm over your head and lean over to the right side of your body. Return to original position and repeat stretch to the left side of your body. Do this for a total of eight times for each side.

Upper Body Twist

Stand with your feet shoulder-width apart and both arms straight out in front of you. Twist your upper body to the right and swing both arms as far right as you can. Turn to the left in the same manner. Repeat for a total of eight times for each side.

Neck Stretch

With your hands on hips, tilt your head down slowly until your chin touches your chest. Rotate your head 360° slowly to the right two times. Stop and rotate your head two times to the left. Repeat for a total of eight times.

Back and Abdomen Stretch

Lie on your stomach and grab your ankles. Pull yourself up by raising your head and feet together. Repeat for a total of eight times. Rest for a few second between each raise.

4
Basic Techniques

The basic techniques of Taekwondo are very important, especially for the beginner, since they are the foundation for one's overall knowledge of the martial art. They are also paramount in the overall progress of the practitioner—whether novice or expert. Therefore, it is imperative to constantly review and improve these basic techniques in order to succeed in Taekwondo. The pictures in this chapter show examples of basic stances, blocks, strikes, and kicks used in Taekwondo.

STANCES

Stances are important for good balance, effective strikes, and quick reaction.

Back stance

The feet are one and a half steps apart. Point the front foot forward and the back foot 90° outward. Both knees are slightly bent with both feet flat on the floor. The center of the head, hip, and the heel of the back foot are in alignment. The body weight is distributed 70% on the back leg and 30% on the front leg.

Crane stance

The balancing foot is flat on the floor with knee slightly bent. The other leg is slightly raised with the knee bent at a 40° angle. This stance is used either defensively or offensively as a starting position for the side kick and back kick.

Cross stance

In a cross stance, the legs are positioned so as to form an "X". Place the back foot on the opposite side of the front foot, and lift the back heel 4–5 inches from the floor. The front foot is flat on the floor. Both knees are slightly bent. The body weight is resting 90% on the front leg and 10% on the back leg. This is used as a side attack and defense.

Forward stance

Point the back foot 45° outward. Bring the front foot one and a half steps forward with the toes pointed straight ahead. The back knee is straight while the front knee leg is slightly bent. The balance is at the center of the body.

Horse stance

The feet are a shoulder-width apart. Both knees are slightly bent and flexed inward. Push the chest slightly forward. Have both fists at waist level with wrists facing upward. The point of balance is between the feet.

Kicking stance

Place one foot forward and one foot back, about one step-length apart. The knees are slightly bent with the body positioned sideways to protect its vital points. This position is in preparation to fight and is used in sparring.

Ready stance

The upper body, waist, and knees are straight. Shoulders are relaxed, the chin is pulled in, eyes looking forward, and the feet are spread 1-foot apart with the toes pointing forward. This stance is the starting point for all movements.

Tiger stance

The feet are 1½-foot length apart. Point the front foot forward with its heel 4–5 inches above the floor. The front toes are barely touching the floor. The back foot is flat on the floor. Both knees are slightly bent and flexed slightly inward. The body weight is all on the back leg. The top of the head, hip, and the heel of the back leg are in alignment.

Walking stance

The feet are one step-length apart and pointing forward. Both knees are locked. The body weight is distributed with 70% on the front foot and 30% on the back foot.

BLOCKS

Blocks are direct or circular movements to stop strikes or kicks. Blocks can prevent injury or even save your life. The high block is an upward movement of the arm to deflect a punch to the face or a strike to the head. The low block is a downward movement of the arm to block a strike on either side of the lower body below the navel. The middle block can be inward or outward in a circular movement to protect the middle section of the body—from the collar bone to the navel. A palm block is a downward movement of the open hand to stop a strike or kick. An X-block can be a downward or upward movement with your arms crossed to block a fist, hand strike, and kick.

High block

This block protects the face and top of the head against a strike. Assume a horse stance. The movement starts with the blocking arm down at waist level in front of the body. Swing the arm up, crossing the chest, above the top of the head. Block with the outer wrist.

High X block

Assume a forward stance. Place both fists at the waist. Bring both fists up, crossing at the neck, and straighten the elbows to create a powerful outward movement. This block is used to protect the face and top of the head.

Hinge shape block

Assume a horse stance. Bring one fist to the hip level with palm up. Bring the other fist, with palm down, over to the same side of the body. For a large hinge shape block, the top arm comes across the chest area (as shown in photo). For a small hinge shape block, the top arm is slightly lower to protect the solar plexus.

Low block

Assume a horse stance. Bring the fist of the blocking arm up to the level of the opposite ear. Bring the arm straight down to protect the lower part of body (below the waist). Block with the outer wrist. In a double low block, bring each fist to the level of the opposite ear. Then bring both fists down to protect the lower body.

Low X block

Assume a forward stance. Cross the wrists in front of the abdomen while straightening the elbows as to perform a powerful downward movement. This block is used to protect the lower part of the body (below the waist).

Mountain shape block

Assume a horse stance. Bring both fists up from the side of the body towards the center until the elbows are at shoulder height and the arms are parallel. The palms are facing inward. Block with the wrists. This block is used to defend against an attack to the face by two aggressors.

Outward middle block

Assume a horse stance. Bring the blocking arm from the inside of the body upward and outward until the wrist is at shoulder level. Block with the inner wrist. This block prevents a strike between the shoulders and waist. An inside middle block brings the blocking arm upward to ear level and inward, protecting the solar plexus with the outer wrist. In a double middle block, the other arm is brought up to the middle section of the body for extra protection.

Palm block

Assume a back stance. Bring the palm of the blocking hand from the outside at ear level downward with a powerful movement to the low abdomen. This block is used to protect solar plexus and face.

Wedge block

For an inner wedge block (as shown in the photo), cross the arms in front of the neck with palms facing the body. Then uncross the arms in an upward position until arms are shoulder-width apart. Use the inner arms to block. For an outer wedge block, cross the arms at the wrists in front of the neck with palms facing the body. Then uncross by rotating the wrists outward so that the palms point downward and the fists are shoulder-width apart. Use the outer wrists to block. This block is used defend a hit or grab to the chest, shoulders, and neck.

Strikes and kicks are circular or direct movements targeted at the opponent's body. Strikes include fist punches, hammer fist, fingertip strikes, knife-hand, palm strike, knee strike, elbow strike, and head butting. Kicks include the front snap kick, jumping front snap kick, stretching kick, ax kick, roundhouse kick, fast roundhouse kick, jumping roundhouse kick, side kick, sliding side kick, flying side kick, inside and outside crescent kicks, back kick, spinning back kick, hook kick, spinning hook kick, jumping spinning hook kick, flying scissors kick (see back cover), and pushing kick.

Ax kick

This kick can be performed two ways: either by bending the knee while lifting up the leg or keeping a straight knee while lifting up the leg. To execute a bent knee ax kick, chamber the knee against the chest. Unfold and swing the leg in a downward position using the hip to create power. To execute a straight knee ax kick, follow the same movement but keep the knee straight. This kick is mostly used in sparring for strikes to the head and shoulder.

Crescent kick

This kick can be performed two ways: inner crescent kick or outer crescent kick. Lock the knee while lifting up the leg and kicking in an inward (with the sole of the foot) or outward (with the side of the foot) semi-circle. The photo shows an inner crescent kick. This kick is used to block a hand attack, as a strike to the side of the face, or simply to stretch.

Elbow strike

Assume a forward stance. Bend the elbow and place the fist of the striking elbow in the opposite hand in order to add more power to the strike. Hit with the flat part of the elbow—not the tip. This strike is mostly used when the attacker is close. It can be used upward to the chin, downward to a knee, or outward to the torso.

Fingertip strike

Assume a horse stance. Form a spear by extending the striking arm with fingers together and thumb tucked in. The tip of the fingers are slightly bent inward. It is used for a thrusting attack to the eyes, throat, solar plexus, or abdomen. Alternative strikes include the straight spear finger, upper spear finger, and flat spear finger, depending upon the hand's direction.

Fist punch

Assume a horse stance. Bring the fist of the punching arm upward and straighten the elbow to form a powerful forward movement directed to a specific target.

Front snap kick

Assume a walking stance. Kick directly in front of you with a straight leg while pointing the toes forward and using the top of the foot to strike. Return to a ready position for a counterattack. This kick can also be done using the sole or instep of the foot. In these two cases, point the toes upward and bend the knee. This kick is used to strike the face, solar plexus, groin area, and front of the knee.

Hammer fist/Back fist

A hammer fist and back fist look similar, but are done differently. For a hammer fist, assume a ready stance. Place the fist of the striking arm against the opposite shoulder with palm inward and elbow bent. Rotate the fist like the second hand of a clock until the elbow is straightened. This powerful strike is used to attack the top of the head, face, shoulders, chest, sides, and arms.

For a back fist, the beginning stance and position of the arm is the same. Instead of rotating the fist, direct the arm outward, hitting with the back of the fist. This is used to attack the face, side of the head, and solar plexus. In a double back fist, the other fist is in a guarded position. The elbow is bent at 90° and the arm is across the body.

Knee strike

Bend the knee while using the hip to create the upward thrust. It is used to attack the face, solar plexus, abdomen, and genital area.

Knife-hand

Assume a horse stance. Swing the palm of the striking hand down or out (as shown in photo) to block a strike or kick. The knife-hand strike can also be used to attack the neck, face, and the back of the head. It can also be used to block an attack to the torso. It is often used when breaking boards. In a double knife-hand, the other hand is palm up and horizontal to the chest for protection.

Palm strike

Assume a forward stance. Snap up the palm of the striking hand. This is mostly used to throw the head of the opponent back by striking from under the chin. It may also be used to target the face, chest, solar plexus, or abdomen.

Pull move/Uppercut punch

Assume a back stance. Use the pulling arm to pull the back of the opponent's head towards you. This move is usually accompanied by an uppercut punch in which the other arm then throws an upward punch to the opponent's face or side.

Roundhouse kick

Chamber the knee against the chest and simultaneously pivot the opposite foot 180°. Using the instep, strike the face, stomach, or rib/kidney area. This kick is frequently used in Taekwondo because of its power, accuracy, and simplicity.

Side kick

Chamber the knee against the chest and thrust it toward the target in a direct, linear movement. Use the heel and the outer edge of the foot to strike.

Spinning back kick

Pivot 180° on the ball of the standing front leg while chambering the back leg. Quickly look over your shoulder as you turn to catch the opponent's movement. Turn the body slightly toward the target, and strike with the heel in a direct, linear movement.

Spinning hook kick

Pivot 360° on the ball of the standing front leg while chambering the rear leg. As the body spins around, release the kicking leg in a circular and upward motion, attacking the face area with the sole of the foot. This kick must be done quickly and accurately in order to be efficient and powerful.

Stretching kick

Kick the leg up into a vertical position. Lock the knee and hit with the sole or ball of the foot. This kick is mostly used to condition the muscles for more strenuous kicks and as a defensive move in sparring.

5
Forms

Forms are offensive and defensive moves put together in sequences. They contain fundamental stances, blocks, kicks, and punches. During this process, certain parts of the body are transformed into weapons. The purpose of forms is to help the student develop good reflexes for sparring. In other words, forms are the basic training for sparring.

Taekwondo has three types of forms for students under the first degree black belt: two *Kibon* forms, eight *Taegeuk* forms, and eight *Palgwe* forms. The main purpose of *Kibon* is to develop the basic stances and coordination of the beginner. It introduces the novice to imaginary attacks.

Taegeuk is a more advanced type of form on which the basics of Taekwondo are built. It represents the most profound Eastern philosophy from which the views of the world, cosmos, and life are derived. *Tae* in *Taegeuk* means "bigness" while *Geuk* means "eternity." Therefore, *Taegeuk* has no form, no beginning, and no end. In short, everything comes from *Taegeuk* and *Taegeuk* contains the essence of everything. Out of *Taegeuk* comes eight branches of philosophical theories, which are discussed later.

Palgwe is a form that symbolically expresses all the phenomena of man and the universe. It contains all mutually contradictory concepts, which are forever developing and growing by combining and changing. The sky and the earth, light and darkness, good and evil, man and woman are all universal phenomena meeting and departing from one another according to certain rules. The *Palgwe* applies this mysterious and profound Eastern philosophy to the movements of Taekwondo. With this, the students comprehend the basic principles of Taekwondo, which are composed of change and cooperation, conflict and harmony.

Advanced forms for students who hold black belts are: *Koryo* (Korea), *Keumgang* (Diamond), *Taebaek* (no English translation), *Pyongwon* (Plain), *Sipjin* (Decimal), *Jitae* (Earth), *Cheonkwon* (Sky), *Hansoo* (Water), and *Ilyo* (Oneness). The meaning of these advanced forms are described later.

Kibon Form I *(Kibon El-Jon)*

1 Starting in a ready stance on the center of the line (D1-C1 at point B), turn to the left (90º) while sliding the left foot into a left forward stance and executing a low block with the left arm.

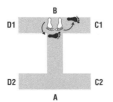

2 Move the right foot one step forward and execute a middle section straight punch with the right hand.

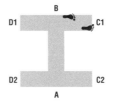

3 Pivoting on the ball of the left foot, turn to the right (180º toward D1) while sliding the right foot into a right forward stance and executing a low block with the right arm.

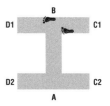

4 Move the left foot into a left forward stance and execute a middle section straight punch with the left hand.

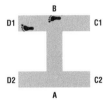

5 Pivoting on the ball of the right foot, turn to the left (90° toward A) while sliding the left foot into a left forward stance and executing a low block with the left hand.

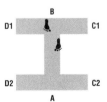

6 Move the right foot into a right forward stance and execute a middle section straight punch with the right hand.

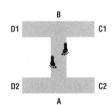

7 Move the left foot into a left forward stance and execute a middle section straight punch with the left hand.

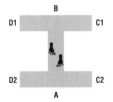

8 Move the right foot into a right forward stance and execute a middle section straight punch with the right hand. Yell!

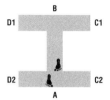

9 Pivoting on the ball of the right foot, turn to the left (270° on D2) while sliding the left foot into a left forward stance and executing a low block with the left hand.

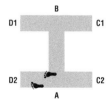

10 Move the right foot into a right forward stance and execute a middle section straight punch with the right hand.

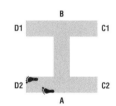

11 Pivoting on the ball of the left foot, turn to the right (180° toward C2) into a right forward stance while executing a low block with the right arm.

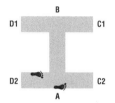

12 Move the left foot into a left forward stance while executing a middle section straight punch with the left hand.

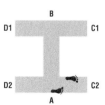

14 Move the right foot into a right forward stance and execute a middle section straight punch with the right hand.

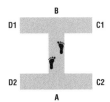

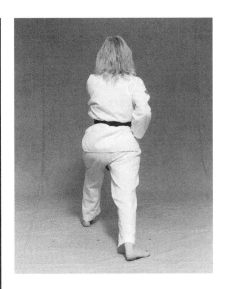

13 Pivoting on the ball of the right foot, turn to the left (90° toward B) while moving into a left forward stance and executing a low block with the left hand.

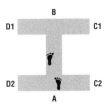

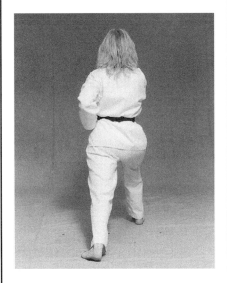

15 Move the left foot into a left forward stance and execute a middle section straight punch with the left hand.

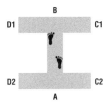

16 Move the right foot into a right forward stance while executing a middle section straight punch with the right hand. Yell. Pivoting on the ball of the right foot, turn left (180°) into the starting position.

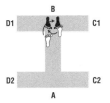

KIBON Form 2 *(Kibon E-Jang)*

1 Starting in a ready stance on the center of the line (D1-C1 at point B), turn to the left (90° on C1) while sliding the left foot into a left forward stance and executing a middle section outer block with the left arm.

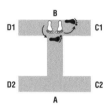

2 Execute a middle section front snap kick with the right foot and drop into a right forward stance followed immediately by a middle section straight punch with the right hand.

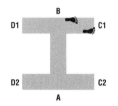

3 Turn to the right (180° toward D1) while sliding the right foot into a right forward stance and executing a middle section outer block with the right arm.

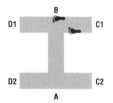

4 Execute a middle section front snap with the left foot and drop into a left forward stance while executing a middle section straight punch with the left hand.

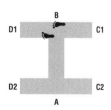

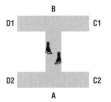

7 Move the left foot into a left forward stance while executing a middle section straight punch with the left hand.

6 Move the right foot into a right forward stance while executing a middle section straight punch with the right hand.

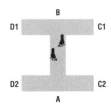

5 Turn to the left (90° toward A) while sliding the left foot into a left forward stance and executing a low block with the left hand.

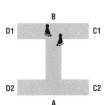

8 Move the right foot into a right forward stance while executing a middle section straight punch with the right hand. Yell.

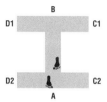

9 Pivoting on the ball of the right foot, turn to the left (270° on D2) while sliding the left foot into a left forward stance and executing a middle section outer block with the left hand.

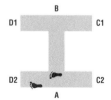

10 Execute a middle section front snap kick with the right foot and drop into a right forward stance followed immediately by a middle section straight punch with the right hand.

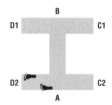

11 Pivoting on the ball of the left foot, turn to the right (180° toward C2) into a right forward stance while executing a middle section outer block with the right arm.

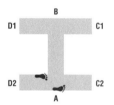

12 Execute a middle section front snap kick with the left foot and drop into a left forward stance followed immediately by a middle section straight punch with the left hand.

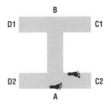

13 Pivoting on the ball of the right foot, turn around to the left (90° toward B) into a left forward stance while executing a left low block.

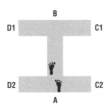

14 Move the right foot into a right forward stance while executing a middle section straight punch with the right hand.

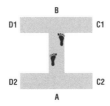

15 Move the left foot into a left forward stance while executing a middle section straight punch with the left hand.

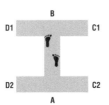

16 Move the right foot into a right forward stance while executing a middle section straight punch with the right fist. Yell. Pivoting on the ball of the right foot, turn left (180°) into the starting position.

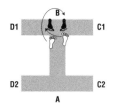

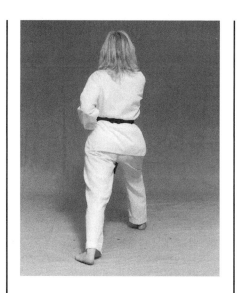

TAEGEUK
The Universal Symbol of Harmony

Harmony is created by an equal balance between two opposite forces.

TAEGEUK

Taegeuk Form 1 (*Jang*)

Taegeuk 1 Jang applies a series of actions of *keon* (heaven) of palgwe, which is the principal of eight *gwes* (eternity). Taegeuk is the source of everything, beginning with *keon*. From heaven comes the light and the rain—both necessary for nature to start, grow, and continue. *Keon* represents creation on earth while the *gwe* represent its continuity. Man starts his life on earth but continues it everlasting in heaven. The eight trigrams express symbolically all phenomena of man, nature, and the universe. Taegeuk 1 applies to the walking stance, forward stance, middle punch, middle block, and front snap kick, which are combined to help the student understand their underlying philosophy.

TAEGEUK Form I (*Tae Geuk El-Jong*)

1 Starting in a ready position on the center of line (D1-C1 at point B), turn 90° to the left while moving your left foot into a left walking stance and executing a low block with the left arm.

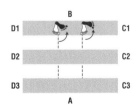

2 Move the right foot into a right walking stance while executing a middle section punch with the right fist.

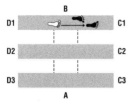

3 Pivoting on the ball of the left foot, turn to the right (180° facing D1). Move the right foot into a right walking stance while executing a low block with the right arm.

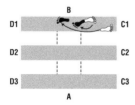

4 Move the left foot into a left walking stance while executing a middle section punch with the left fist.

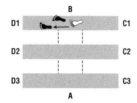

5 Turn to the left (90° facing A) while sliding the left foot into a left forward stance and executing a low block with the left arm.

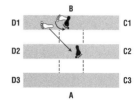

6 Remain in the same position and execute a punch to the middle section with a right fist.

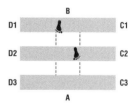

7 Step to the right (90° facing D2) with the right foot into a right walking stance while executing an inside middle block with the left arm.

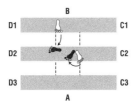

8 Step forward with the left foot into a left walking stance while executing a middle section punch with a right fist.

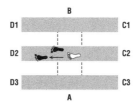

9 Step to the left (180° facing C2) with the left foot into a left walking stance while executing an inside middle block with the right arm.

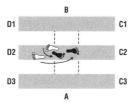

10 Step forward with right foot into a right walking stance while executing a middle section punch with left fist.

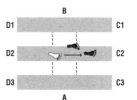

11 Turn to the right (90° facing A) with right foot into a right forward stance while executing a low block with right arm.

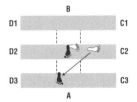

12 Remain in the same position and execute a punch to the middle section with left fist.

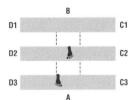

13 Step to the left (90° facing C3) into a left walking stance while executing a high block with the left arm.

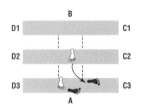

14 Keeping the left foot in place, execute a middle section front kick with the right foot. Step down into a right walking stance and execute a middle section punch with the right fist.

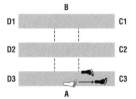

15 Turn to the right (180° facing D3) with the right foot into a right walking stance while executing a high block with the right arm.

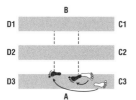

16 Keeping the right foot in place, execute a middle section front kick with the left foot. Step down into a left walking stance while executing a middle section punch with the left fist.

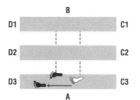

17 Step to the right (90° facing B) with the left foot into a left forward stance while executing a low section block with the left hand.

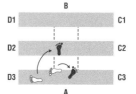

SIDE VIEW

18 Step forward with the right foot into a right forward stance while executing a middle section punch with the right fist. Yell. Turn left (180°) by pivoting on the right foot to end in a ready position.

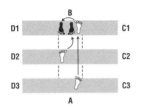

SIDE VIEW

Taegeuk Form 2 (*Jang*)

Taegeuk 2 Jang applies a series of actions of joyfulness (*Tae*) of Palgwe. It begins with a low block, a middle punch, a front snap kick, and ends with a face block. This is a state in which one's mind is kept strong although it appears gentle. Therefore, smile and virtue will prevail. These actions are performed gently but forcefully so that there is force behind the softness.

TAEGEUK Form 2 *(Tae Geuk E-Jang)*

1 Starting in a ready position on the center of line (D1-C1 at point B), turn 90° to the left while sliding the left foot into a left walking stance and executing a low block with the left arm.

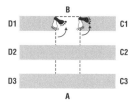

2 Move the right foot into a right forward stance while executing a middle section straight punch with the right hand.

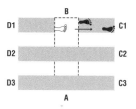

3 Pivoting on the ball of the left foot, turn to the right (180° toward D1) while sliding the right foot into a right walking stance and executing a low block with the right arm.

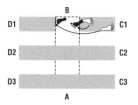

4 Move the left foot into a left forward stance while executing a middle section straight punch with the left hand.

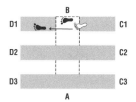

5 Pivoting on the ball of the right foot, turn to the left (90° toward A) while sliding the left foot into a left walking stance and executing a middle section inside block with the right hand.

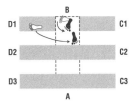

6 Move the right foot into a right walking stance while executing a middle section inside block with the left hand.

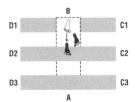

7 Pivoting on the ball of the right foot, turn to the left (90° toward C2) by moving the left foot into a left walking stance and execute a low section block with the left hand.

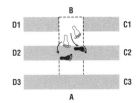

8 With the left foot fixed, execute a middle section front snap kick with the right foot. Drop into a right forward stance while executing a high section straight punch with the right hand.

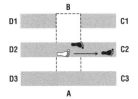

9 Pivoting on the ball of the left foot, turn to the right (180° toward D2) while sliding the right foot into a right walking stance and executing a low section block with the right hand.

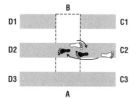

10 With the right foot fixed, execute a middle section front snap kick with the left foot and drop into a left forward stance while executing a high section straight punch with the left fist.

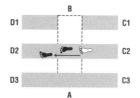

11 Pivoting on the ball of the right foot, turn to the left (90° toward A) by moving the left foot into a left walking stance and execute a high section block with the left arm.

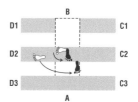

12 With the left foot fixed, move the right foot one step forward into a right walking stance while executing a high section block with the right arm.

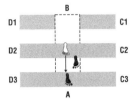

13 Pivoting on the ball of the right foot, turn to the left (270° toward D3) by moving the left foot into a left walking stance and execute a middle section inside block with the right hand.

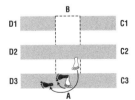

14 Pivoting on the ball of the left foot, turn to the right (180° toward C3) by moving the right foot into a right walking stance and execute a middle section inside block with the left hand.

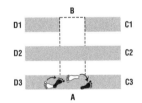

15 Pivoting on the ball of the right foot, turn the left (90° toward B) by moving the left foot into a left walking stance and execute a low section block with the left hand.

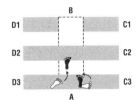

16

With the left foot fixed, execute a middle section front snap kick with the right foot and drop into a right walking stance while executing a middle section straight punch with the right fist.

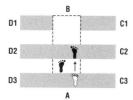

SIDE VIEW

SIDE VIEW

17 With the right foot fixed, execute a middle section front snap kick with left foot and drop into a left walking stance while executing a middle section straight punch with the left fist.

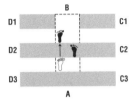

SIDE VIEW

SIDE VIEW

18 With the left foot fixed, execute a middle section front snap kick with the right foot and drop into a right walking stance while executing a middle section straight punch with the right fist. Yell. Pivoting on the ball of the right foot, turn to the left (180° facing A) and assume the ready position.

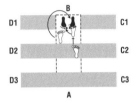

SIDE VIEW

SIDE VIEW

Taegeuk Form 3 *(Jang)*

This symbol means fire and sun. It distinguishes man from animal, since man can use fire. Burning fire gives man light, warmth, enthusiasm, and hope. These Taegeuk actions are performed with variety and passion. They are based on low block, front snap kick, punch, middle knife block, and neck attack with hand knife. They apply the principle of Palgwe and help the practitioner attain vigor.

TAEGEUK Form 3 (*Tae Geuk Sam-Jang*)

1 Starting in a ready position on the center of line (D1-C1 at point B), turn to the left (90°) by moving the left foot into a left walking stance and executing a low section block with the left arm.

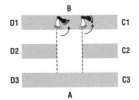

2 With the left foot fixed, execute a middle section front snap kick with the right foot and drop into a right forward stance while executing a middle section double punch starting with the right fist.

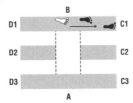

3 Pivoting on the ball of the left foot, turn to the right (180° toward D1) by moving the right foot into a right walking stance and executing a low section block with the right arm.

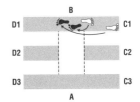

4 With the right foot fixed, execute a middle section front snap kick with the left foot and drop into a left forward stance while executing a middle section double punch starting with the left fist.

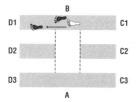

5 Turn to the left (90° toward A) by moving the left foot into a left walking stance while executing a high section inward knife-hand strike (neck level) with the right hand.

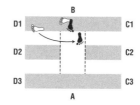

6 With the left foot fixed, step forward into a right walking stance while executing an inward knife-hand strike to the high section with the left hand.

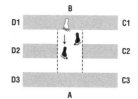

7 Turn to the left (90° toward C2) by moving the left foot into a right back stance while executing a middle section knife-hand block with the left hand.

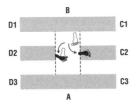

8 Slide the left foot into a left forward stance while executing a middle section punch with the right fist.

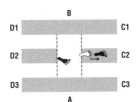

9 Pivoting on the ball of the left foot, turn to the right (180° toward D2) by moving the right foot into a left back stance while executing a middle section knife-hand block with the right hand.

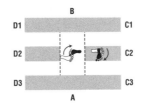

10 Slide the right foot into a right forward stance while executing a middle section punch with the left fist.

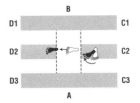

11 Turn to the left (90° toward A) by moving the left foot into a left walking stance while executing a middle section inside block with the right arm.

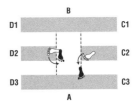

13 Pivoting on the ball of the right foot, turn to the left (270° toward D3) by moving the left foot into a left walking stance while executing a low section block with the left arm.

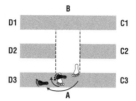

12 Step forward with the right foot into a right walking stance while executing a middle section inside block using the left arm.

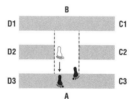

14 With the left foot fixed, execute a middle section front snap kick with the right foot and drop into a right forward stance while executing a middle section double punch starting with the right fist.

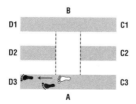

15 Pivoting on the ball of the left foot, turn to the right (180° toward C3) by moving the right foot into a right walking stance while executing a low section block with the right arm.

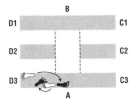

16 With the right foot fixed, execute a middle section front snap kick with the left foot and drop into a left forward stance while executing a middle section double punch starting with the left fist.

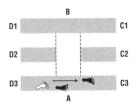

17 Turn to the left (90° toward B) by moving the left foot into a left walking stance while executing a low section block with the left arm. Follow immediately with a middle section straight punch with the right fist.

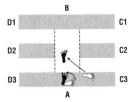

SIDE VIEW

18 With the left foot fixed, move the right foot one step forward into a right walking stance while executing a low section block with the right arm. Follow immediately with a middle section straight punch with the left fist.

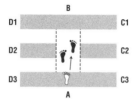

SIDE VIEW

SIDE VIEW

SIDE VIEW

19 With the right foot fixed, execute a middle section front snap kick with the left foot and drop into a left walking stance while executing a low section block with the left arm. Follow immediately with a middle section straight punch with the right fist.

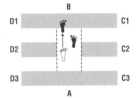

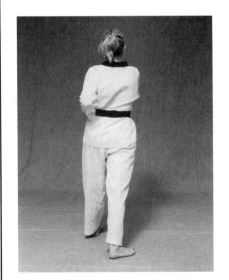

SIDE VIEW

SIDE VIEW

SIDE VIEW

20 With the left foot fixed, execute a middle section front snap kick wit the right foot and drop into a right walking stance while executing a low section block with the right arm. Follow immediately with a middle section straight punch with the left fist. Yell. Pivoting on the ball of the right foot, turn to the left (180° toward A) and return to the ready stance.

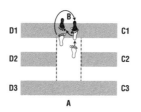

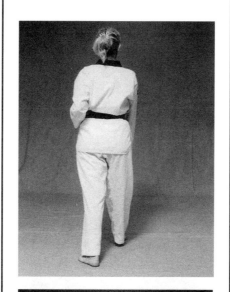

SIDE VIEW

SIDE VIEW

SIDE VIEW

Taegeuk Form 4 (*Jang*)

Taegeuk 4 Jang symbolizes thunder, the object of fear and trepidation. This principle suggests that one should remain calm and brave in the face of danger in order for the blue sky and the sunlight to reappear. It applies the *Jin* principle of Palgwe. Its actions consist of knife block, fingertip strike, face block, punch, outside middle block, inside middle block, side kick, and front snap kick.

TAEGEUK Form 4 (*Tae Geuk Sa-Jang*)

1 Starting in a ready position on the center of line (D1-C1 at point B), turn to the left (90° toward C1) by moving the left foot into a right back stance while executing a left double knife-hand block.

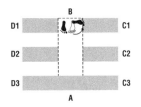

2 Move the right foot into a right forward stance while executing a palm block with the left hand. Follow immediately with a middle section fingertip strike with the right hand.

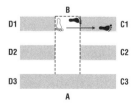

3 Turn to the right (180° toward D1) by moving the right foot into a left back stance while executing a right double knife-hand block.

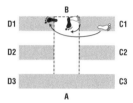

4 Move the left foot into a left forward stance while executing a palm block with the right hand. Follow immediately with a middle section fingertip strike with the left hand.

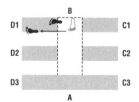

5 Turn to the left (90° toward A) by moving the left foot into a left forward stance while executing a high section knife-hand strike with the right hand and a high section block with the left knife-hand (a swallow shape knife-hand neck strike).

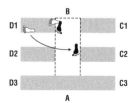

6 With the left foot fixed, execute a middle section front snap kick with the right foot. Step down with the right foot into a right forward stance while executing a middle section straight punch with the left fist.

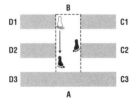

7 Using the right foot as the axis, execute a middle section side kick with the left foot.

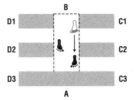

8 Step down and quickly pivot on the ball of the left foot to execute a middle section side kick with the right foot. Step down with the right foot into a left back stance while executing a middle section double knife-hand block.

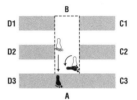

9 Pivoting on the ball of the right foot, turn left (270° toward D3) by moving the left foot into a right back stance while executing an outward middle block with the left arm.

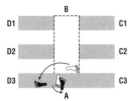

10 Execute a middle section front snap kick with the right foot. Step back into a right back stance while executing inside arm block with the right arm.

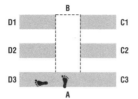

11 Pivoting on the ball of the left foot, turn to the right (180° toward C3) by moving the right foot into a left back stance while executing an outside middle block.

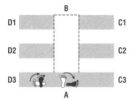

12 Execute a middle section front snap kick with the left foot. Step back with the left foot to assume a left back stance while executing an inside middle block with the left arm.

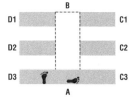

SIDE VIEW

13 Pivoting on the ball of the right foot, turn to the left (90° toward B) by moving the left foot into a left forward stance while executing a swallow shape knife-hand neck strike with the left hand and a high section block with the right hand.

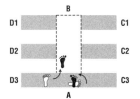

SIDE VIEW

14 With the left foot fixed, execute a middle section front snap kick with the right foot and step down into a right forward stance while executing a right strike back fist with the right hand.

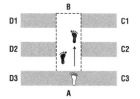

SIDE VIEW

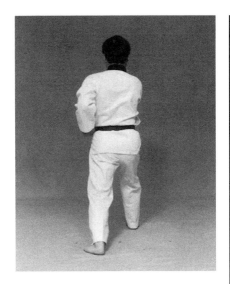

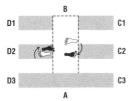

Pivoting on the ball of the left foot, turn to the right (180° toward C2) by moving the right foot into a right walking stance while executing an inside middle block with the right arm.

FRONT VIEW

16 Keeping both feet fixed, execute a middle section punch with the right fist.

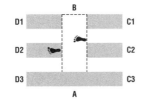

15 Pivoting on the ball of the right foot, turn to the left (90° toward D2) by moving the left foot into a left walking stance while executing an inside middle block with the left arm.

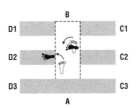

18 Keeping both feet fixed, execute a middle section punch with the left arm.

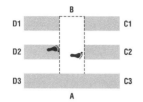

19 Turn to the left (90° toward B) by sliding the left foot into a left forward stance while executing an inside middle block using the left arm. Remaining in the same stance, execute a middle section double punch starting with the right fist.

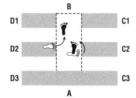

SIDE VIEW   SIDE VIEW   SIDE VIEW

20 With the left foot fixed, step forward by sliding the right foot into a right forward stance while executing an inside middle block with the right arm. Remaining in the same stance, execute a middle section double punch starting with the left fist. Yell with the last punch. Pivoting on the ball of the right foot, turn to the left (180° toward A) by moving your left foot into the ready stance.

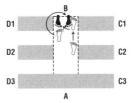

SIDE VIEW

SIDE VIEW

SIDE VIEW

Taegeuk Form 5 (*Jang*)

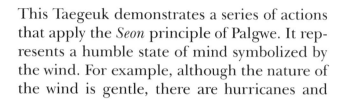

This Taegeuk demonstrates a series of actions that apply the *Seon* principle of Palgwe. It represents a humble state of mind symbolized by the wind. For example, although the nature of the wind is gentle, there are hurricanes and tornadoes. Actions might proceed gently and monotonously as a breeze. Yet, at other times, it may start as forcefully as a storm. The actions of this form consist of hammer fist, elbow strike, and back fist.

TAEGEUK Form 5 (*Tae Geuk O-Jang*)

1 Starting in the ready position on the center of line (D1-C1 at point B), turn to the left (90° toward C1) by moving the left foot into a left forward stance while executing a low block with the left arm.

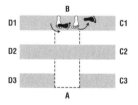

2 Slide back the left foot into an open stance while executing a downward hammer fist strike with the left hand.

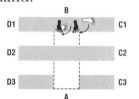

3 Turn to the right (90° toward D1) by moving the right foot into a right forward stance while executing a low block with the right arm.

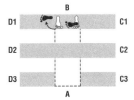

4 Slide the right foot back into an open stance while executing a downward hammer fist strike with the right hand.

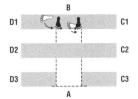

5 Step forward (toward A) with the left foot into a left forward stance while executing an outward middle block with the left arm. Remain in the same stance and immediately execute a second outward middle block with the right arm.

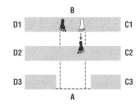

6 With the left foot fixed, execute a middle section front snap kick with the right foot and step down into a right forward stance while executing a high section back-fist strike with the right hand. Remain in the same stance and execute an outward middle block with the left arm.

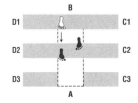

8 With the left foot fixed, step forward with the right foot into a right forward stance while executing a high section (side of the head) back-fist strike with the right hand.

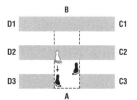

7 With the right foot fixed, execute a middle section front snap kick with the left foot and step down into a left forward stance while executing a high section back-fist strike with the left hand. Remain in the same stance and execute an outward middle block with the right arm.

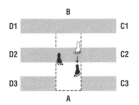

9 Pivoting on the ball of the right foot, turn to the left (270° toward D3) by moving the left foot into a right back stance while executing a middle section single knife-hand block with the left hand.

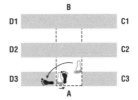

10 With the left foot fixed, cover the knuckles of the right fist with the left knife-hand and move the right foot forward into a right forward stance in order to execute an elbow strike with the right elbow.

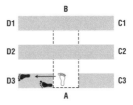

11 Pivoting on the ball of the left foot, turn to the left (180° toward C3) by moving the right foot into a left back stance while executing a single knife-hand block with the right hand.

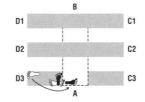

12 Cover the knuckles of the left fist with the right hand-knife and move the left foot forward into a left forward stance in order to execute an elbow strike with the left elbow.

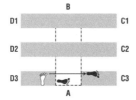

13 Turn to the left (90° toward **B**) by sliding the left foot into a left forward stance while executing a low block with the left arm. Remain in the same stance and execute a middle section outer block with the right arm.

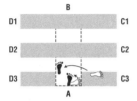

SIDE VIEW

SIDE VIEW

14

With the left foot fixed, execute a middle section front snap kick with the right foot and step down into a right forward stance while executing a low block with the right arm. Remain in the same stance and execute a middle section inside block with the left arm.

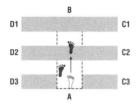

SIDE VIEW

SIDE VIEW

SIDE VIEW

15 Pivoting on the ball of the right foot, turn to the left (90° toward D2) by moving the left foot into a left forward stance while executing a high block with the left arm.

16 With the left foot fixed, execute a middle section side kick with the right foot. Step down into a right forward stance while executing a middle section left elbow strike to the palm of the right hand.

17 Pivoting on the ball of the left foot, turn to the right (180° toward C2) by moving the right foot into a right forward stance while executing a high block with the right arm.

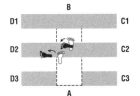

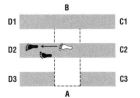

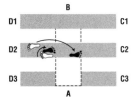

18 With the right foot fixed, execute a middle section side kick with the left foot. Step down into a left forward stance while executing a middle section right elbow strike to the palm of the left hand.

19 Turn to the left (90° toward B) by sliding the left foot into a left forward stance while executing a low block with the left arm. Remain in the same stance and execute an outward middle block with the right arm.

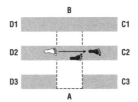

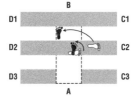

SIDE VIEW

SIDE VIEW

20 Execute a middle section front snap kick with the right foot and jump forward into a right cross stance while executing a high section (side of the head) back-fist strike with the right hand. Yell. Pivoting on the ball of the right foot, turn to the left (180° toward A) into a ready position.

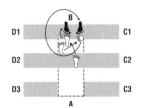

SIDE VIEW

SIDE VIEW

Taegeuk Form 6 (*Jang*)

This form's principle teaches the lesson that anyone can overcome obstacles and hardships if one proceeds with self-confidence. It applies the *Gam* principle of Palgwe, which means water. Water is formless and never loses its nature. This illustration is characterized by *Momtong-Bakat-Makki* and five actions in which *Sonnal-Eolgool-Makki* is executed by twisting the body in *Jebipoom* actions.

TAEGEUK Form 6 (*Tae Geuk Yook-Jang*)

1 Starting in a ready position on the center of line (D1-C1 at point B), turn to the left (90° toward C1) by moving the left foot into a left forward stance and executing a low block with the left arm.

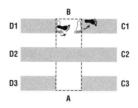

2 Execute a middle section front snap kick with the right foot. Step back with the right foot into a right back stance while executing an outer arm block with the left arm.

3 Pivoting on the ball of the left foot, turn to the right (180° toward D1) by moving the right foot into a right forward stance while executing a low block with the right arm.

4 Execute a middle section front snap kick with the left foot. Step back with the left foot into a left back stance while executing an outer arm block with the right arm.

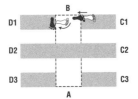

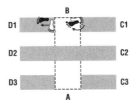

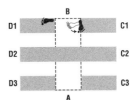

5 Turn to the left (90° toward A) by sliding the left foot into a left forward stance while executing a body twist knife-hand block with the right hand.

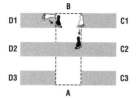

7 Step down into an open stance, then move the left foot into a left forward stance while executing an outer block to the face with the left arm. Then execute a middle section straight punch with the right fist.

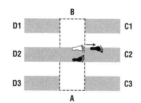

6 With the left foot fixed, execute a middle section round kick with the right foot.

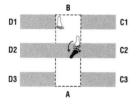

8 With the left foot fixed, execute a middle section front snap kick with the right foot. Step down into a right forward stance while executing a middle section straight punch with the left fist.

9 Pivoting on the ball of the left foot, turn to the right (180° toward D2) by moving the right foot into a right forward stance while executing an outer block to the face with the right arm. Execute a middle section straight punch with the left hand.

10 With the right foot fixed, execute a middle section front snap kick with the left foot. Step down into a left forward stance while executing a middle section punch with the right fist.

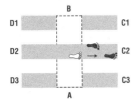

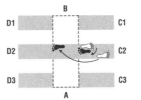

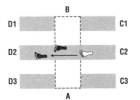

11 Turn to the left (90° toward A) by moving the left foot into an open stance crossing your arms under the chin. Lower your arms slowly in front of your body, then execute a low section open block with both arms.

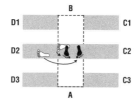

12 With the left foot fixed, move the right foot into a right forward stance while executing a body twist knife-hand block with the left hand.

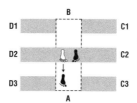

13 With the right foot fixed, execute a middle section round kick with the left foot. Yell.

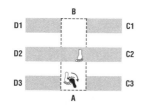

14 Step down with the left foot. Pivoting on the ball of the right foot, turn right (180° toward C3) by moving the right foot into a right forward stance while executing a low section block with the right arm.

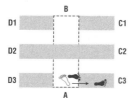

15 Execute a middle section front snap kick with the left foot. Step back into a left back stance while executing an outer arm block with the right arm.

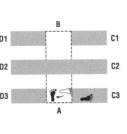

16 Pivoting on the ball of the right foot, turn to the left (180° toward D3) by moving the left foot into a left forward stance while executing a low section block with the left arm.

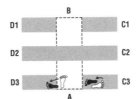

17 Execute a middle section front snap kick with the right foot. Step back into a right back stance while executing an outer arm block with the left arm.

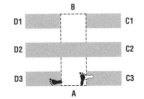

18 Pivoting on the ball of the left foot, turn to the right (90° toward A) into a right back stance while executing a double knife-hand block.

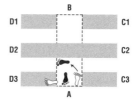

19 Move the left foot back into a left back stance while executing a double knife-hand block.

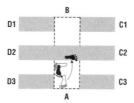

20 Step back with the right foot into a left forward stance while executing a middle section palm block with the left hand.

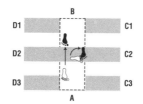

21 Remain in the same stance and execute a middle section punch with the right fist.

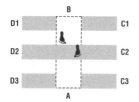

22 With the right foot fixed, step back with the left foot into a right forward stance while executing a middle section palm block with the right hand.

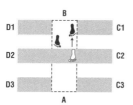

23 Remain in the same stance and execute a middle section straight punch with the left fist. With the left foot fixed, move the right foot back and assume the ready stance.

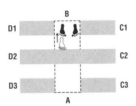

Taegeuk Form 7 (*Jang*)

In this form, the *Gan* principle of Palgwe is applied by a series of actions. *Gan* means the "top stop" and symbolizes a mountain. The message carried here is that one should stop when one first could, and one should go forward when one must. In order to achieve something, moving and stopping should be synchronized. Since a mountain never moves, one should learn its stability and not act in a hasty manner. Though fast actions seem fine, we should know when and where to stop.

TAEGEUK Form 7 *(Tae Geuk Chil-Jang)*

1 Starting in a ready position on the center of line (D1-C1 at point B), turn to the left (90° toward C1) by moving the left foot into a left tiger stance while executing a palm block with the right hand.

2 With the left foot fixed, execute a middle section front snap kick with the right foot. Step back into a left tiger stance while executing an inner arm block with the left arm.

3 Turn to the right (180° toward D1) by moving the right foot into a right tiger stance while executing a palm block with the left hand.

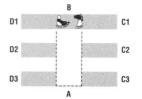

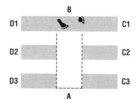

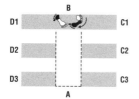

4 Execute a middle section front snap kick with the left foot. Step back into a right tiger stance while executing an inner arm block with the right arm.

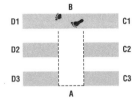

5 Turn to the left (90° toward A) by moving the left foot into a right back stance and executing a low section double knife-hand block.

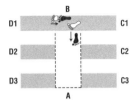

6 Step forward into a left back stance while executing a low section double knife-hand block.

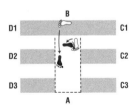

7 Turn to the left (90° toward C2) by moving the left foot into a left tiger stance while executing a palm block with the right hand and moving the left fist under the right elbow.

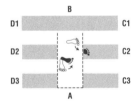

8 Remain in the same stance and execute a high section back-fist strike with the right fist.

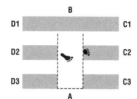

9 Pivoting on the ball of the left foot, turn to the right (180° toward D2) by moving the right foot into a right tiger stance while executing a palm block with the left hand and moving the right fist under the left elbow.

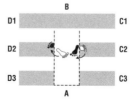

10 Remain in the same stance and execute a high section back-fist strike with the left fist.

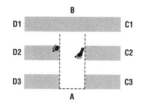

11 Pivoting on the ball of the left foot, turn to the left (90° toward A) into a close stance and place the left palm over the knuckles of the right fist. Raise the fist slowly to the chin level at half arm's length in front of the body.

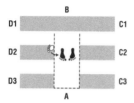

12 With the right foot fixed, step forward the left foot (toward A) into a left forward stance while simultaneously executing an outer arm block with the left arm and a low block with the right arm. Remaining in the same stance, execute an outer arm block with the right arm and a low block with the left arm.

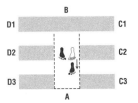

13 With the left foot fixed, move the right foot into a right forward stance while simultaneously executing an outer arm block with the right arm and a low block with the left arm. Remaining in the same stance, execute an outer arm block with the left arm and a low block with the right arm.

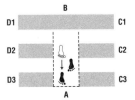

14 Pivoting on the ball of the right foot, turn left (270° toward D3) into a left forward stance while executing an outer wedge block using both arms.

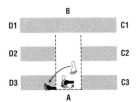

15 Execute a middle section knee strike with the right knee. Jump forward into a right cross stance while executing a middle section uppercut knuckle punch with both hands.

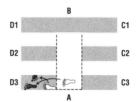

16 Keeping the right foot fixed, step back with the left foot into a right forward stance while executing a low section X block.

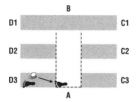

17 Pivoting on the ball of the left foot, turn right (180° toward C3) with the right foot into a right forward stance while executing an outer wedge block with both arms.

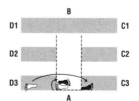

18 Execute a middle section knee strike with the left knee. Jump forward into a left cross stance while executing a middle section uppercut knuckle punch with both hands.

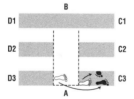

19 Keeping the left foot fixed, step back with the right foot into a left forward stance while executing a low section X block.

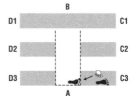

20 Pivoting on the ball of the right foot, turn left (90° toward B) into a left walking stance while executing a high section side back-fist strike with the left hand.

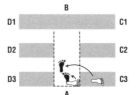

SIDE VIEW

21 Execute an inner crescent kick with the right foot to the left palm. Step down into a horse stance and execute an elbow strike to the left hand's palm with the right elbow.

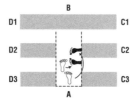

SIDE VIEW

23 Execute an inner crescent kick with the left foot to the right palm. Step down into a horse stance while executing an elbow strike to the right hand's palm's with the left elbow (front view).

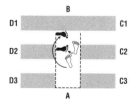

22 Keeping the right foot fixed, slide the left foot back into a right walking stance while executing a high section (side of the head) side back-fist with the right hand.

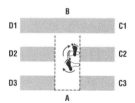

SIDE VIEW

24 Keeping both feet fixed, execute a single knife-hand block with the left hand.

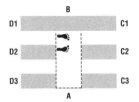

SIDE VIEW

25 With the left foot fixed, close the left hand into a fist (grabbing the opponent) and move the right foot in front (180° toward D1) into a horse stance while executing a middle section side punch with the right fist. Yell. Pivoting on the ball of the right foot, turn the body to the left and assume a ready stance.

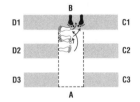

SIDE VIEW

Taegeuk Form 8 (*Jang*)

Taegeuk 8 Jang applies the *Gon* principle of Pal-gwe. It symbolizes the earth, which is the source of life. All things take life from the earth, grow from it, and draw limitless amount of energy from it. The earth is where all creative forces of heaven are embodied. With this form, all fundamental actions are brushed up and reviewed before the first Dan (black belt).

1 Starting in a ready position on the center of the line (D1-C1 at point B, facing A), move the left foot one step forward into a right back stance while executing a double outer arm-block. Slide the left foot into a left forward stance while executing a middle section punch with the right fist.

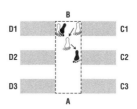

2 Execute a jumping front snap kick with the left foot and yell. Land onto a left forward stance while executing an inner arm block with the left forearm. Execute two rapid middle section punches starting with the right fist.

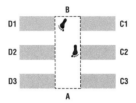

3 With the left foot fixed, step forward with the right foot into a right forward stance while executing a middle section straight punch with the right fist.

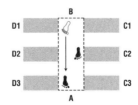

4 Pivoting on the ball of the right foot, turn to the left (180° facing D3) by moving the left foot in a circle manner to form a right forward stance. Simultaneously execute an outer arm block with the right forearm and a low block with the left forearm.

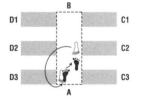

5 Twist the body left to change the stance into a left forward stance while executing an uppercut punch with the right fist and bringing the left fist to the right shoulder.

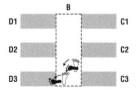

6 Move the left foot behind the right foot and quickly twist the upper body to the right. Then step out with the right foot to form a left forward stance while simultaneously executing an outer arm block with the left arm and a low block with the right arm.

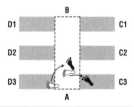

7 Twist the body to the right to form a right forward stance while executing an uppercut punch with the left fist and bringing the right fist to the left shoulder.

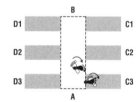

8 Pivoting on the ball of the left foot, turn to the left (180° facing D3) by moving the right foot into a right back stance while executing a double knife-hand block.

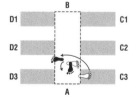

9 Slide the left foot into a left forward stance while executing a middle section punch with the right fist.

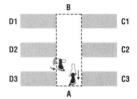

10 Execute a middle section front snap kick with the right foot. Drop the right foot back to its original position and step back with the left foot into a right tiger stance while executing a middle section palm block with the right hand.

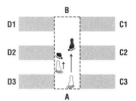

11 Turn left (90° facing C2) by moving the left foot into a left tiger stance while executing a middle section double knife-hand block.

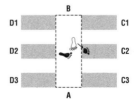

12 With the right foot fixed, execute a middle section front snap kick with the left foot. Step down into a left forward stance while executing a middle section punch with the right fist.

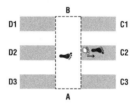

13 Slide the left foot back into a left tiger stance while executing a middle section palm block with the left hand.

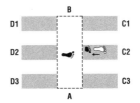

14 Turn right (180° toward D2) with the right foot into a right tiger stance while executing a double knife-hand block.

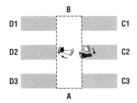

15 With the left foot fixed, execute a front snap kick with the right foot. Step down into a right forward stance while executing a middle section straight punch with the left fist.

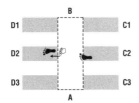

16 With the left foot fixed, slide the right foot back into a right tiger stance while executing a middle section palm block with the right hand.

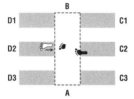

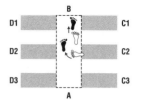

17 Pivoting on the ball of the left foot, turn to the right (90° facing B) by moving the right foot into a left back stance while executing a low block with the right hand and protecting the solar plexus with the left fist.

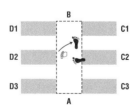

SIDE VIEW

18 Execute a middle section front snap kick with the left foot. Jump into the air and while both feet are off the floor, execute a high section front kick with the right foot. Land on a right forward stance while executing an inner arm block with the right arm. Follow immediately with a middle section punch with the left fist. Yell.

SIDE VIEW

SIDE VIEW   SIDE VIEW   SIDE VIEW

19 Pivoting on the ball of the right foot, turn to the left (270° facing C1) by moving the left foot into a right back stance while executing a middle section knife-hand with the left hand.

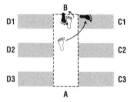

20 With the right foot fixed, slide the left foot forward into a left forward stance while executing a high section elbow strike with the right elbow.

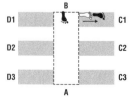

21 Remain in the same stance and execute a high section backfist strike with the right fist. Follow immediately with a middle section straight punch with the left fist.

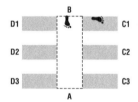

22 With the left foot fixed, turn to the right (180° facing D1) by pulling the right foot back into a left back stance while executing a middle section knife-hand block with the right hand.

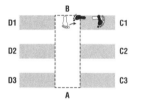

23 Slide the right foot forward into a right forward stance while executing a high section elbow strike with the left elbow.

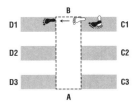

24 Execute a high section back-fist strike with the left fist. Follow immediately with a middle section punch with the right fist. Yell. With the right foot fixed, move the left foot toward the right foot into a ready stance.

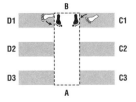

PALGWE Form I *(Palgwe El-Jang)*

1 Starting in a ready position on the center of the line (D1-C1 at point B,

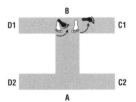

facing A), turn to the left (90° toward C1) and slide the left foot into a left forward stance while executing a low block with the left arm.

2 Slide the right foot into a right forward stance and execute a middle section outer block with the right arm.

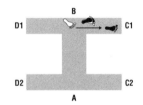

3 Pivoting on the ball of the left foot, turn right (180° facing D1) by moving the right foot into a right forward stance while executing a low block with the right arm.

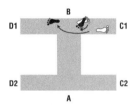

4 With the right foot fixed, slide the left foot into a left forward stance and execute a middle section outer block with the left arm.

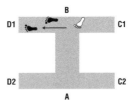

5 Pivoting on the ball of the right foot, turn left (90° facing A) by moving the left foot into a left forward stance while executing a low block with the left arm.

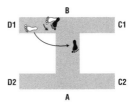

6 With the left foot fixed, move the right foot forward into a left back stance while executing a middle block to the inside with the right arm.

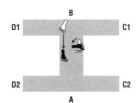

7 With the right foot fixed, move the left foot forward into a right back stance while executing a middle block to the inside with the left arm.

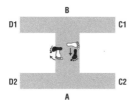

8 With the left foot fixed, slide the right foot forward into a right forward stance while executing a middle section straight punch with the right fist. Yell.

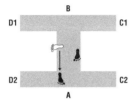

9 Pivoting on the ball of the right foot, turn to the right (270° facing D2) by sliding the left foot into a right back stance while executing a double knife-hand block to the middle section.

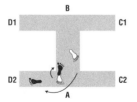

10 With the left foot fixed, move the right foot forward into a left back stance while executing a middle block to the inside section with the right arm.

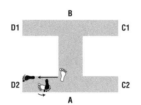

11 Pivoting on the ball of the left foot, turn to the right (180° facing C2) by sliding the right foot forward into a left back stance while executing a double knife-hand block to the middle section.

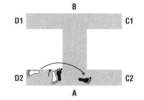

12 With the right foot fixed, move the left foot forward into a right back stance while executing a middle block to the inside section with the left hand.

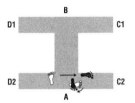

13 Pivoting on the ball of the right foot, turn left (90° facing B) by sliding the left foot into a left forward stance while executing a low block with the left arm.

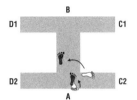

SIDE VIEW

14 With the left foot fixed, move the right foot forward into a right forward stance while executing a right knife-hand to the high section (neck).

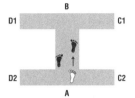

SIDE VIEW

15 With the right foot fixed, move the left foot forward into a left forward stance while executing a left knife-hand to the high section.

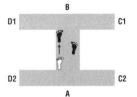

SIDE VIEW

16 With the left foot fixed, move the right foot into a right forward stance while executing a middle section punch with the right fist. Yell.

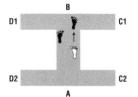

SIDE VIEW

17 Pivoting on the ball of the right foot, turn to the left (270° facing C1) by moving the left foot into a left forward stance while executing a low block with the left arm.

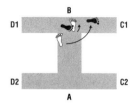

18 With the left foot fixed, move the right foot into a right forward stance while executing a middle block to the inside section with the right arm.

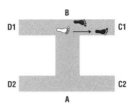

19 Pivoting on the ball of the left foot, turn right (180° facing D1) by sliding the right foot into a right forward stance while executing a low block with the right arm.

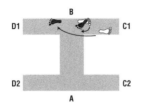

20 With the right foot fixed, move the left foot into a left forward stance while executing a middle block to the inside section with the left arm. Turn to the left (90° facing B) and assume the ready position.

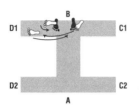

PALGWE Form 2 (*Palgwe E-Jang*)

1 Starting in a ready position on the center of the line (D1-C1 at point B, facing A), turn left (90°) by sliding the left foot into a left forward stance while executing a high block with the left hand.

2 With the left foot fixed, execute a front snap kick with the right foot and step down into a right forward stance while executing a straight punch to the middle section with the right fist.

3 Pivoting on the ball of the left foot, turn right (180° facing D1) by moving the right foot into a right forward stance while executing a high block with the right hand.

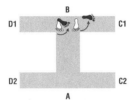

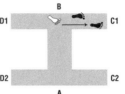

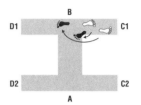

4 With the right foot fixed, execute a front snap kick to the middle section with the left foot and step down into a left forward stance while executing a straight punch to the middle section with the left fist.

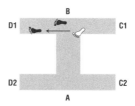

5 Pivoting on the ball of the right foot, turn left (90° facing A) by moving the left foot into a right back stance while executing a low double knife-hand.

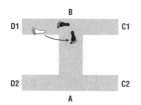

6 With the left foot fixed, move the right foot forward into a left back stance while executing a double knife-hand to the middle section.

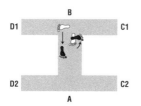

7 With the right foot fixed, move the left foot into a left forward stance while executing a left high block with the left hand.

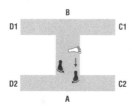

8 With the left foot fixed, move the right foot into a right forward stance while executing a middle section straight punch with the right fist.

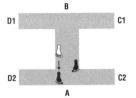

9 Pivoting on the ball of the right foot, turn to the left (270° facing D2) by moving the left foot into a left forward stance while executing a left high block with the left arm.

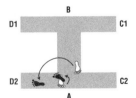

10 With the left foot fixed, execute a front snap kick to the middle section with the right foot. Step down into a right forward stance while executing a straight punch to the middle section with the right fist.

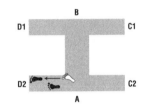

11 Pivoting on the ball of the left foot, turn to the right (180° facing C2) by moving the right foot into a right forward stance while executing a high block with the right hand.

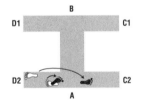

12 With the right foot fixed, execute a front snap kick to the middle section with the left foot and step down into a left forward stance while executing a middle section punch with the left fist.

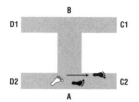

13 Pivoting on the ball of the right foot, turn left (90° facing B) by moving the left foot into a right back stance while executing a low double-hand block.

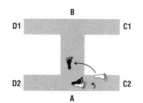

SIDE VIEW

14 With the left foot fixed, move the right foot forward into a left back stance while executing a double outward middle block with the right arm.

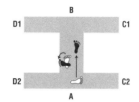

SIDE VIEW

15 With the right foot fixed, move the left foot forward into a right back stance while executing an outward middle block with the left arm.

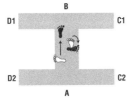

SIDE VIEW

16 With the left foot fixed, move the right foot forward into a right forward stance while executing a middle section punch with the right fist.

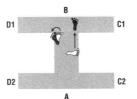

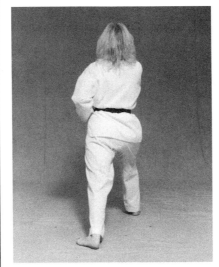

SIDE VIEW

17 Pivoting on the ball of the right foot, turn left (270° facing C1) by moving the left foot into a left forward stance executing a left high block with the right arm.

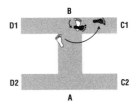

18 With the left foot fixed, execute a middle section front snap kick with the right foot. Step down into a right forward stance while executing a middle section punch with the right fist.

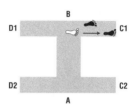

19 Pivoting on the ball of the left foot, turn right (180° facing D1) by moving the right foot into a right forward stance while executing a high block with the right arm.

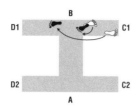

20 With the right foot fixed, execute a middle section front snap kick with the left foot. Step down into a left forward stance while executing a middle section straight punch with the left fist. Turn to the left (90° facing A) and resume your original position.

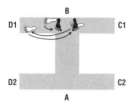

PALGWE Form 3 *(Sam-Jang)*

1 Starting in a ready position on the center of the line (D1-C1 at point B, facing A), turn to the left (90° facing C1) and slide the left foot into a left forward stance while executing a low block with the left arm.

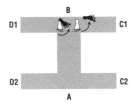

2 With the left foot fixed, move the right foot into a right forward stance while executing a middle section straight punch with the right fist.

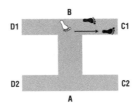

3 Pivoting on the ball of the left foot, turn right (180° facing D1) by moving the right foot into a right forward stance while executing a low block with the right hand.

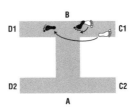

4 With the right foot fixed, move the left foot into a left forward stance while executing a middle section straight punch with the left fist

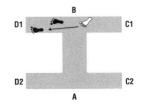

5 Pivoting on the ball of the right foot, turn to the left (90° toward A) by moving the left foot into a left forward stance while executing a low block with the left arm.

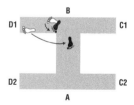

6 With the left foot fixed, move the right foot into a right forward stance while executing a high block with the right arm.

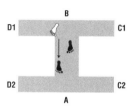

7 With the right foot fixed, move the left foot into a left forward stance while executing a high block with the left arm.

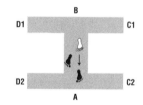

8 With the left foot fixed, move the right foot into a right forward stance while executing a high section straight punch with the right fist.

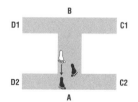

9 Pivoting on the ball of the right foot, turn left (270° facing D2) by moving your left foot into a right back stance while executing a double knife-hand block.

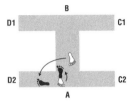

10 With the left foot fixed, move the right foot forward into a left back stance while executing a double knife-hand block.

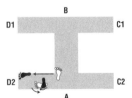

11 Pivoting on the ball of the left foot, turn right (180° facing C2) by moving the right foot into a left back stance while executing a double knife-hand block.

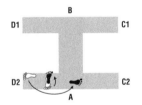

12 With the right foot fixed, move the left foot forward into a right back stance while executing a double knife-hand block.

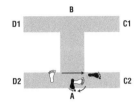

13 Pivoting on the ball of the right foot, turn left (90° facing B) by moving the left foot into a right back stance while executing a double knife-hand block.

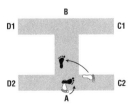

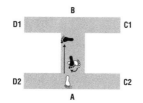

15 With the left foot fixed, move the right foot backward into a right back stance while executing an inside middle block with the left arm.

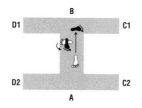

14 Leaving your feet in the same spot, turn the body to the right (180° toward A) by moving the right foot into a left back stance while executing an outward middle block with the right arm.

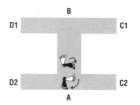

16 Move the left foot backward into a left back stance while executing an inside middle block with the right arm.

17 Move the right foot backward into a right back stance while executing an inside middle block with the left arm.

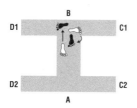

18 Leaving your feet in the same spot, turn the body to the right (180° facing B) by moving the right foot into a left back stance while executing an outward middle block with the right arm.

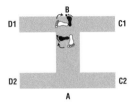

19 Pivoting on the ball of the right foot, turn the body to the left (270° toward C1) by moving the left foot into a left forward stance while executing a high block with the left arm.

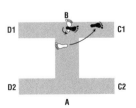

20 With the left foot fixed, move the right foot into a right forward stance while executing a high section punch with the right fist.

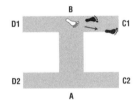

21 Pivoting on the ball of the left foot, turn right (180° toward D1) by moving the right foot into a right forward stance while executing a high block with the right arm.

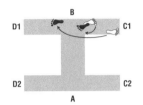

22 Move the left foot forward into a left forward stance while executing a high section punch with the left fist. Turn left and return to original position (90° facing A).

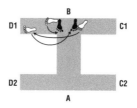

PALGWE Form 4 *(Sa-Jang)*

1 Starting in a ready position on the center of the line (D1-C1 at point B, facing A), turn left (90° facing C1) by moving the left foot into a right back stance while simultaneously executing an outward middle section block with the left arm and a high block with the right arm.

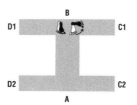

2 Keeping the body in the same position, execute a pull move (of the head) with the left hand and an upper punch with the right fist.

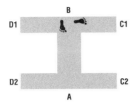

3 Keeping the right foot fixed, pull the left foot back into a ready stance while executing a outer knife-hand with the left arm.

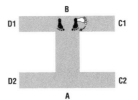

4 Turn the body to the right (90° facing D1) by moving the right foot into a left back stance while simultaneously executing an outward middle section block with the right arm and a high block with the left arm.

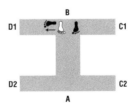

5 Keeping the body in the same position, execute a pull move (of the head) with the right hand and an upper punch with the left fist.

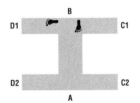

6 Keeping the left foot fixed, pull the right foot back into a ready stance while executing an outward knife-hand with the right arm.

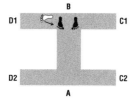

7 Move the left foot forward into a right back stance while executing a double knife-hand.

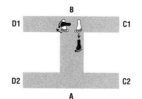

8 With the left foot fixed, execute a high-section front snap kick with the right foot. Step down into a right forward stance while executing a palm block with the left hand and a fingertip strike with the right hand.

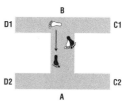

9 Leaving your feet in the same spot, twist your upper body back while pulling your right hand back to the right side of your body. Immediately bring your left foot into a left forward stance (180° facing A) while executing an outer hammer fist with the left arm.

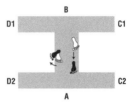

10 With the left foot fixed, move the right foot forward into a right forward stance while executing a middle section punch with the right fist.

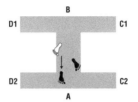

11 Pivoting on the ball of the right foot, turn the body to the left (270° facing D2) by moving the left foot into a right back stance while executing an outward middle block with the left hand and high block with the right arm.

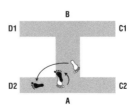

12 Keeping the feet in the same position, execute a pull move (of the head) with the right hand and an upper punch with the left fist.

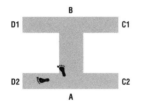

13 Keeping the right foot fixed, pull the left foot back into a ready stance while executing an outer knife-hand strike with the left arm.

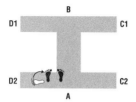

14 Turn the body to the right (90° facing C2) by moving the right foot into a left back stance while executing a right middle section outer block with the right arm and a high block with the left arm.

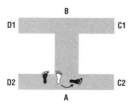

15 Keeping the feet in the same position, execute a pull move (of the head) with the right hand and an upper punch with the left fist.

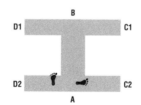

16 Keeping the left foot fixed, pull the right foot back into a ready stance while executing an outer knife-hand with the right arm.

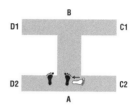

17 Move the left foot one step forward into a right back stance while executing a double knife-hand.

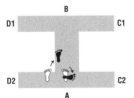

18 Execute a high section front snap kick with the right foot. Step down into a right forward stance while executing a palm block with the left hand and a fingertip strike with the right hand.

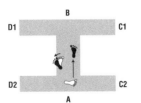

19 Leaving your feet in the same spot, twist your upper body back while pulling your right hand to the right side of the head. Immediately bring your left foot into a left forward stance (180° facing B) while executing an outer hammer fist with the left arm.

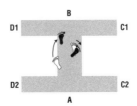

SIDE VIEW

20 With the left foot fixed, move the right foot into a right forward stance while executing a middle section straight punch with the right fist.

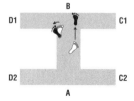

21 Pivoting on the ball of the right foot, turn the body to the left (180° facing A) by moving the left foot into a horse stance while executing a low block with the left arm.

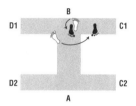

22 Shift your feet into a left forward stance while executing a middle section straight punch with the right fist.

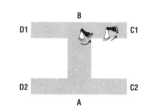

23 Keeping the right foot in place, pull the left foot into a horse stance while executing a low block with the right hand. Shift your feet into a right forward stance while executing a middle section straight punch with the left arm. Return to the original position.

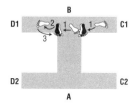

PALGWE Form 5 *(O-Jang)*

1 Starting in a ready position on the center of the line (D1-C1 at point B, facing A), move the left foot back into a right forward stance while executing a low block with the right wrist and a middle section block with the left wrist (scissors block).

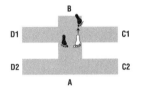

2 With the right foot fixed, move the left foot to the left (90° facing C1) into a right back stance while executing a left low-section double knife-hand block.

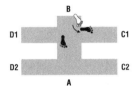

3 Pivoting on the ball of the left foot, move the right foot forward into a left back stance while executing a right middle-section double knife-hand block.

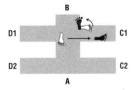

4 With the left foot fixed, move the right foot forward into a right back stance while executing a middle section palm block with the left hand.

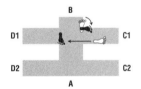

5 With the left foot fixed, move the right foot into a right forward stance while executing a middle section straight punch with the right fist.

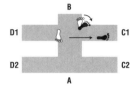

7 Pivoting on the ball of the right foot, move the left foot forward into a right back stance while executing a left middle-section double knife-hand block.

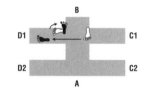

6 Pivoting on the ball of the left foot, turn to the right (180° facing D1) by moving the right foot into a left back stance while executing a right low-section double knife-hand block.

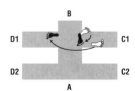

8 Pivoting on the ball of the right foot, move the left foot one step back into a left back stance while executing a middle section palm block with the right hand.

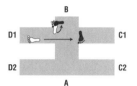

9 With the right foot fixed, move the left foot into a left forward stance while executing a middle section punch with the left fist.

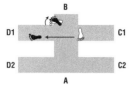

10 Pivoting on the ball of the right foot, turn to the left (90° facing A) by moving the left foot into a left forward stance while executing a low section block with the left wrist and a middle section block with the right wrist (scissors block).

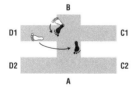

11 With the left foot fixed, move the right foot into a right forward stance while executing an outward middle block with the right hand.

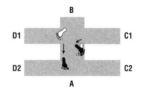

12 With the right foot fixed, move the left foot into a left forward stance while executing an outward middle block with the left hand.

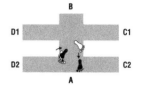

13 With the left foot fixed, move the right foot into a right forward stance while executing a middle section palm block with the left hand and a fingertip strike with the right hand.

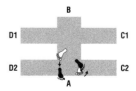

14 Pivoting on the ball of the right foot, turn the body to the left (270° toward D2) by moving the left foot into a left forward stance while executing an outward middle block with the left hand.

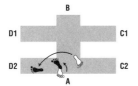

15 Keeping both feet fixed, execute a middle section straight double punch starting with the right fist.

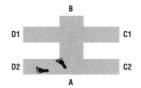

16 Keeping the right foot fixed, lift up the left foot to the knee level and assume a right crane stance. Move the left fist to the right side of the body with the palm toward the body over the right fist.

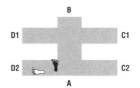

17 With the right foot fixed, execute a side kick with the left foot. Land in a left forward stance while executing a right elbow strike.

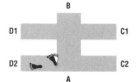

18 Pivoting on the ball of the left foot, move the right foot forward into a left back stance while executing a right middle-section double knife-hand block.

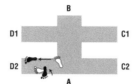

19 Pivoting on the ball of the left foot, turn to the right (180° toward C2) by moving the right foot into a right forward stance while executing an outward middle block with the right arm.

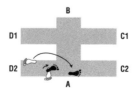

20 Keeping the same stance, execute a middle section straight double punch starting with the left fist.

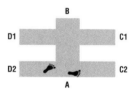

22 With the left foot fixed, execute a right side kick. Land into a right forward stance while executing a left elbow strike.

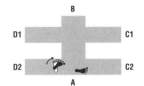

23 Pivoting on the ball of the right foot, move the left foot forward into a right back stance while executing a left middle section double knife-hand block.

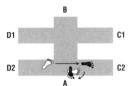

21 Keeping the left foot fixed, lift up the right foot to the knee level and assume a left crane stance. Move the right fist to the left side of the body with the palm toward the body over the left fist.

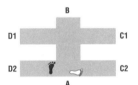

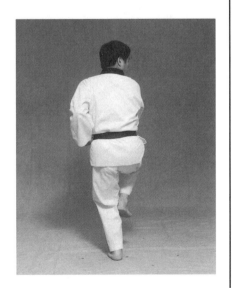

24 Pivoting on the ball of the right foot, turn to the left (90° toward B) by moving the left foot into a left forward stance while executing a low block with the left wrist and a middle section block with the right wrist (scissors block).

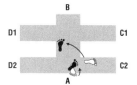

25 Pivoting on the ball of the left foot, move the right foot forward into a left back stance while executing a double low block with the right arm.

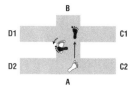

SIDE VIEW

26 Pivoting on the ball of the right foot, move the left foot forward into a right back stance while executing a left wrist guarding low-section block.

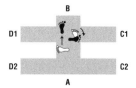

27 Pivoting on the ball of the left foot, move the right foot into a right forward stance while executing a middle section straight punch with the right fist.

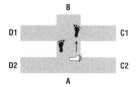

28 Pivoting on the ball of the right foot, turn to the left (270° toward C1) by moving the left foot into a right back stance while executing a left low section knife-hand block.

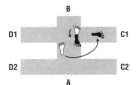

29 Pivoting on the ball of the left foot, move the right foot forward into a left back stance while executing a right middle section double knife-hand block.

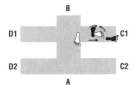

30 With the left foot fixed, move the right foot back into a right back stance while executing a middle section palm block with the left hand.

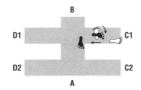

31 Pivoting on the ball of the left foot, move the right foot into a right forward stance while executing a middle section straight punch with the right fist.

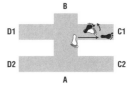

32 Pivoting on the ball of the left foot, turn to the right (180° facing D1) by moving the right foot into a left back stance while executing a right low-section knife-hand block.

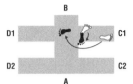

33 Pivoting on the ball of the right foot, move the left foot forward into a right back stance while executing a left middle section knife-hand block.

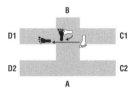

34 Pivoting on the ball of the right foot, move the left foot back into a right back stance while executing a middle section palm block with the right hand.

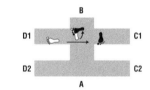

35 With the right foot fixed, move the left foot into a left forward stance while executing a middle section straight punch with the left fist. Turn left (180° facing A) and assume ready position.

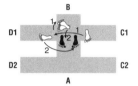

PALGWE Form 6 (*Yook-Jang*)

1 Starting in the ready position on the center of the line (D1-C1 at point B, facing A), turn left (90° toward C1) by moving the left foot into a left back stance while executing a middle section double knife-hand.

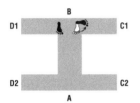

2 Execute a middle section front snap kick with the right foot. Step down into a right forward stance while executing a middle section straight punch with the right fist.

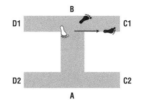

3 Pivoting on the ball of the left foot, turn the body to the right (180° facing D1) by moving the right foot into a left back stance while executing a middle section double hand-knife.

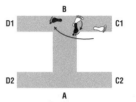

4 With the right foot fixed, execute a middle section front snap kick with the left foot. Step down into a left forward stance while executing a middle section straight punch with the left fist.

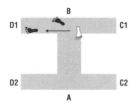

5 Pivoting on the ball of the right foot, turn to the left (90° facing A) by moving the left foot into a left forward stance while executing a low block with the left arm.

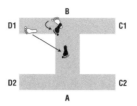

6 Keeping your feet fixed, twist your torso slightly to the left. Raise the left hand with palm out in front of the head for a block (rising knife block) while simultaneously executing a knife-hand strike (to the neck) with the right hand.

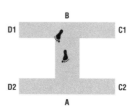

7 With the left foot fixed, execute a high front snap kick with the right foot. As you step down, jump forward with the right foot and move the left foot behind in a cross stance while executing a middle section double-hand back fist.

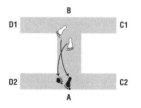

9 Keeping the right foot fixed, slide the left foot into a left forward stance while executing an outer wedge block.

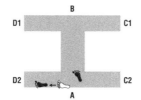

8 Pivoting on the ball of the right foot, turn to the left (270° facing D2) by moving the left foot into a right back stance while executing a low double knife-hand.

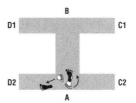

10 With the left foot fixed, execute a front snap kick with the right foot. Step down into a right forward stance while executing a middle section double-punch starting with the right fist.

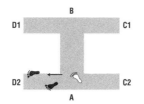

11 Pivoting on the ball of the left foot, turn to the right (180° facing C2) by moving the right foot into a left back stance while executing a low double knife-hand.

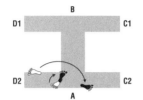

12 Keeping the left foot fixed, slide the right foot into a right forward stance while executing an outer wedge block.

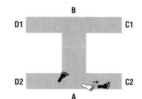

13 With the right foot fixed, execute a middle section front snap kick with the left foot. Step down into a left forward stance while executing a middle section double-punch starting with the left fist.

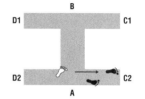

14 Pivoting on the ball of the right foot, turn to the left (90° facing B) by moving the left foot into a right back stance while executing a middle section double knife-hand.

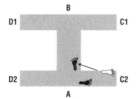

FRONT VIEW

15 Slide the left foot into a left forward stance. Raise the left hand with palm out in front of the head for a block (rising knife block) while simultaneously executing a palm strike with the right hand.

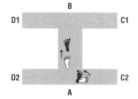

FRONT VIEW

16 With the left foot fixed, execute a high section front snap kick with the right foot. Step down into a right forward stance while executing a back fist with the right hand.

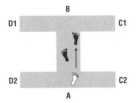

FRONT VIEW

FRONT VIEW

FRONT VIEW

17 With the right foot fixed, execute a high section front snap kick with the left foot. Step down into a left forward stance while executing a high block with the left hand.

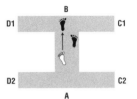

FRONT VIEW

18 With the left foot fixed, execute a middle section side kick with the right foot. Drop down into a left back stance while executing a middle section double knife-hand.

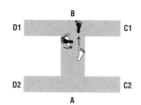

SIDE VIEW

SIDE VIEW

SIDE VIEW

19 Keeping both feet fixed, turn the upper body to the left (180° facing A) into a right back stance while executing a middle section double knife-hand. Return to ready position.

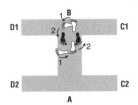

PALGWE Form 7 (*Chil-Jang*)

1 Starting in a ready position at point B, move the left foot into a left forward stance while executing low blocks with both hands.

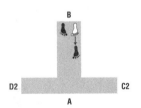

2 With the left foot fixed, execute a high front snap kick with the right foot. Step down into a right forward stance while executing middle section blocks with both hands.

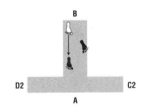

3 With the right foot fixed, execute a front snap kick to the middle section with the left foot. Step down into a left forward stance while executing a high X block.

4 Execute a middle section side kick with the right foot. Step down into a left back stance while executing a middle section double knife-hand.

5 Pivoting on the ball of the right foot, turn to the left (270° facing D2) by moving the left foot into a right back stance while executing an outward middle block with the left hand.

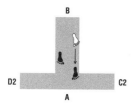

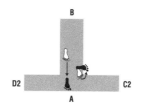

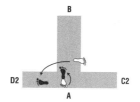

6 With the right foot fixed, move the left foot into a left forward stance while executing a high section straight punch with the right fist.

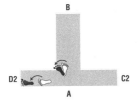

7 Staying in the same stance, execute a high block with the left arm.

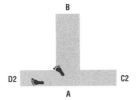

8 Execute a middle section side kick with the right foot. Drop into a left back stance and execute a double knife-hand to the low section.

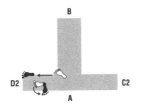

9 Slide the right foot into a right forward stance while executing a middle section straight punch with the left fist.

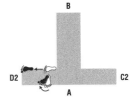

10 Pivoting on the ball of the left foot, turn to the right (180° facing C2) by moving the right foot into a left back stance while executing an outward middle block with the right arm.

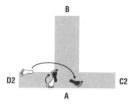

11 With the left foot fixed, move the right foot into a right forward stance while executing a high section straight punch with the left fist.

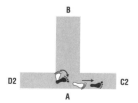

12 Staying in the same stance, execute a high block with the right arm.

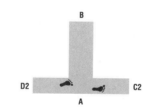

13 Execute a middle section side kick with the left foot. Step down into a right back stance while executing a double knife-hand to the low section.

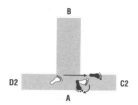

14 With the right foot fixed, move the left foot into a left forward stance while executing a middle section punch with the right fist.

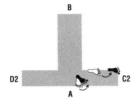

15 Pivoting on the ball of the right foot turn to the left (90° facing B) by moving the left foot into a left forward stance while executing a low X block.

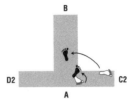

SIDE VIEW

16 Keeping your feet in the same stance, execute a high X block.

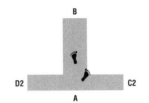

17 Twisting your right hand as if to grab, pull it back toward your body and immediately execute a high section straight punch with the right fist.

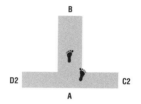

SIDE VIEW

18 Pivoting on the balls of your foot, turn the body to the left (360° facing A) as you shift into a horse stance while executing a low block.

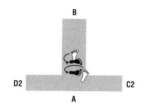

19 With the right foot fixed, twist the upper body to the left and slide the left foot into a left forward stance while executing a high section outer knife-hand with the left hand.

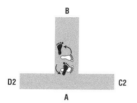

SIDE VIEW

20 Pivoting on the ball of the left foot, turn to the left (90°) while executing a right inner crescent kick to the left palm. Drop the right foot into a horse stance while executing a left elbow strike.

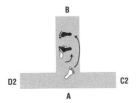

21 Slide right one step sideways while keeping the horse stance position. Execute a side block to high section with the right hand and a side block to the low section with the left hand.

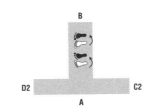

22 Slide sideways to the right once more. Shift your upper body into a right back stance while executing a middle section double knife-hand.

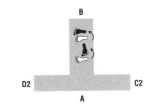

23 Keeping the right foot fixed, move the left foot into a left forward stance while executing a middle section punch with the right fist. Bring the left foot back into a ready position.

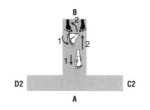

PALGWE Form 8 *(Pul-Jang)*

1 Starting in the ready position on the center of the line (D1-C1 at point B, facing A), turn to the left (90° toward C1) by moving the left foot into a left forward stance while executing a low block with the left hand.

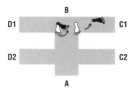

2 Keeping the right foot in place, pull the left foot back into an ease stance while you turn your upper body slightly to the left while executing a left hammer fist.

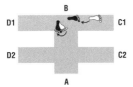

3 With the left foot fixed, move the right foot into a right forward stance (facing C1) while executing a middle section straight punch with the right fist.

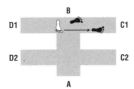

4 Pivoting on the ball of the left foot, turn to the right (180° facing D1) by moving the right foot into a right forward stance while executing a low block with the right hand.

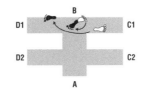

5 Keeping the left foot in place, pull the right foot into an ease stance while you turn your upper body slightly to the right while executing a hammer fist with the right hand.

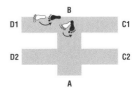

6 With the right foot fixed, move the left foot into a left forward stance (facing D1) while executing a middle section straight punch with the left fist.

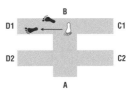

7 Pivoting on the ball of the right foot, turn to the left (90° toward A) by moving the left foot into a right back stance while executing a middle section double hand-knife.

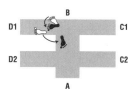

8 With the left foot fixed, move the right foot into a right forward stance while executing palm block with the left hand and a fingertip strike with the right hand.

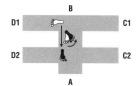

9 Keeping your feet in place, twist your upper body to the left and pull back your right hand to the right side of your body. Pivoting on the ball of the right foot, twist back (180° facing A) and move the left foot into a right back stance while executing a back fist with the left hand.

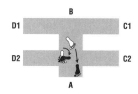

10 With the left foot fixed, move the right foot into a right forward stance while executing a middle section straight punch with the right fist. Yell (kiap).

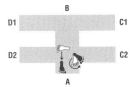

11 Pivoting on the ball of the right foot, turn to the left (270° facing D2) by moving the left foot into a right back stance while executing an outer knife-hand strike with the left hand.

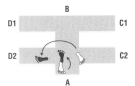

12 With the right foot fixed, bring your left foot back into a horse stance while pulling your left hand toward your chest.

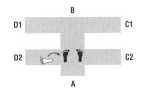

13 With the right foot fixed, move the left foot slightly to the left, still keeping a horse stance, and execute a left elbow strike.

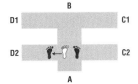

FRONT VIEW

14 With the right foot fixed, turn to the left (90° facing D2) by moving the left foot into a left forward stance while executing a middle section outer block with the left arm.

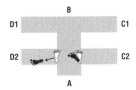

16 With the right foot fixed, turn to the right (90° toward B) by sliding your left foot into a horse stance. Bring the left fist to the left side of your body while the right arm comes across your chest.

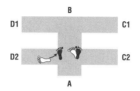

15 Keeping the same stance, execute a middle section straight punch with the right fist.

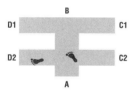

18 With the left foot fixed, bring your right foot back into a horse stance while pulling your hand back toward your chest.

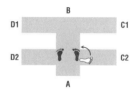

17 With the left foot fixed, turn right (90° facing C2) by moving the right foot into a left back stance while executing an outer knife-hand strike with the right hand.

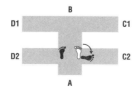

19 With the left foot fixed, move the right foot slightly to the right, still keeping a horse stance, and execute a right elbow strike.

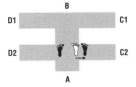

FRONT VIEW

20 Move the right foot into a right forward stance while executing an outward middle block with the right arm.

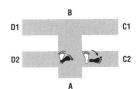

21 Keeping the same stance, execute a middle section punch with the left fist.

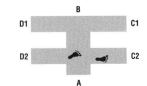

22 Return to a horse stance by turning your body left (90° toward B). Bring your right hand to the right side of your body while your left hand comes across your chest.

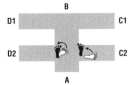

FRONT VIEW

23 Pivoting on the right foot, turn right (90°) and lift your left foot up to the knee level of the right leg.

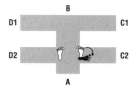

24 Simultaneously execute a side kick with the left foot and a punch with the left fist. Drop into a left forward stance and immediately execute a right elbow strike to the palm of the left hand.

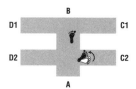

25 Turn the body to the right (90°) by pulling the right foot back into a horse stance. Bring your left hand to the left side of your body while your right arm comes across your chest.

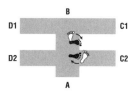

26 Lift your right foot up to the knee level of your left leg.

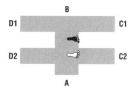

27 Execute a middle section side kick with the right foot as you punch with the right hand. Drop into a right forward stance and immediately execute a left elbow strike to the palm of the right hand.

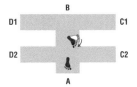

28 Pivoting on the ball of the right foot, turn left (180° facing B) and bring the left foot into a left forward stance while executing a middle section outer block followed by a double upper punch to the ribs.

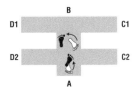

FRONT VIEW

29 Move the right foot into a right forward stance while executing a middle section outer block followed by a double upper punch to the ribs.

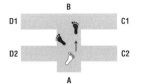

FRONT VIEW

30 Step forward with the left foot into a right back stance while executing a middle section inner knife-hand with the left hand.

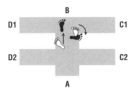

FRONT VIEW

31 Pivoting on the left foot, turn right (180° facing D1) into a horse stance while executing a right elbow strike. Yell.

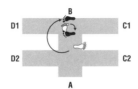

32 Pivoting on the ball of the right foot, turn left (90° facing A) and bring the left foot next to the right. At the chest level, cross your open hands together and slowly point them downward. At halfway to your navel level, snap your hands completely downward in a V shape.

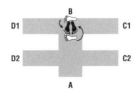

33 With the right foot fixed, move the left foot to the left until you're in a horse stance. Bring the upper arms in line with the shoulders—your fingertips barely touching, and your palms facing down.

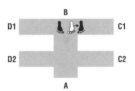

34 Slide to the right, still keeping the horse stance, and execute a left hand punch over the right shoulder.

35 Slide to the left, still keeping the horse stance, and execute a right hand punch over the left shoulder. Yell. Move your left back in and return to original position.

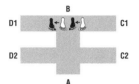

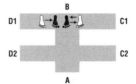

6
Black Belt Forms

Korea *(Koryo Poomse)*

The name of this form comes from an ancient dynasty between 918 and 1392 A.D. in Korea. The English word "Korea" originated from the Koryo Dynasty, which is of great significance to the Korean people. In 1234, Koryo men invented a type of metal new to the world. They also created the famous Koryo ceramics (1398–1468). These precious materials were greatly desired by the Mongolians, who occasionally tried but were unsuccessful in sweeping across the country. This form exemplifies the spirit of the Koryo men. Every motion is a presentation of strong conviction and will, with which the Koryo men held the Mongolians at bay. It shows one's posture in cultivating oneself so that one may follow the wisdom and unyielding spirit of the man of conviction.

Line and Direction of Movement

KOREA

1 Starting in the ready position on the center of the line (D1-C1 at point B, facing A), bring your hands in front of your face, forming a triangle, then step slightly forward. With the right foot fixed, turn to the left (90° facing C1) by sliding your left foot into a right back stance while executing a middle section left double knife-hand block.

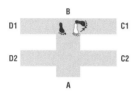

2 Pivoting on the ball of the left foot, turn to the left (180° facing C1) and execute a low section side kick followed by a middle section side kick with the right leg. Drop into a right forward stance while executing an outer knife-hand to the neck.

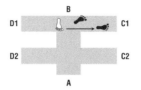

3 Keeping the same stance, execute a middle section straight punch with the left fist.

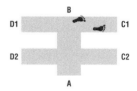

4 Keeping the left foot fixed, move the right foot into a left back stance while executing a middle section inside block with the right hand.

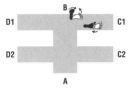

5 Pivoting on the ball of the left foot, turn to the right (180° facing D1) into a left back stance while executing a middle section double knife-hand block with the right hand.

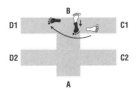

6 Pivoting on the ball of the right foot, turn to the right (180° facing D1) and execute a low section side kick followed by a middle section side kick with the left foot. Drop into a left back stance while executing an outer knife-hand to the neck with the left hand.

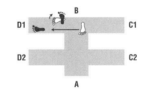

7 Keeping the same stance, execute a middle section punch with the right fist.

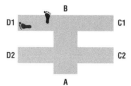

8 Keeping the right foot fixed, move the left foot into a right back stance while executing a middle section inside block with the left hand.

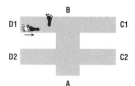

9 Pivoting on the right foot, turn to the left (90° facing A) into a left forward stance while executing a low section knife-hand with the left arm followed by an arc-hand (choking) strike to the neck with the right hand.

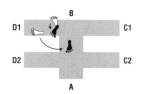

10 Execute a high section front snap kick with the right foot. Drop into a right forward stance while executing a low section knife-hand with the right hand followed by an arc-hand (choking) strike to the neck with the left hand.

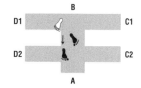

Execute a high section front snap kick with the right foot. Drop into a right forward stance while executing a knee break (low, cupped strike to the knee) with the left hand.

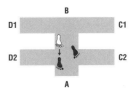

11 Execute a high section front snap kick with the left foot. Drop into a left forward stance while executing a low section knife-hand with the left hand followed by an arc-hand (choking) strike to the neck with the right hand. Yell.

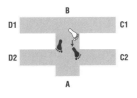

13 Pivoting on the ball of the right foot, turn to the left (180° toward B) into a right forward stance while executing an inner middle section wedge block.

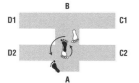

14 Keeping the right foot fixed, execute a middle section front snap kick with the left foot. Drop into a left forward stance while executing a knee break (low, cupped strike to the knee) with the right hand.

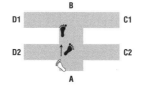

FRONT VIEW

15 Keeping the right foot in place, move the left foot back into a left walking stance while executing an inner middle section wedge block.

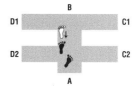

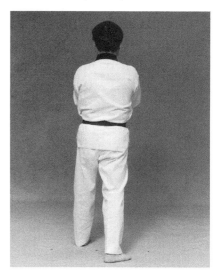

FRONT VIEW

16 Pivoting on the ball of the left foot, turn right (180° facing A) into a horse stance while executing a middle section knife-hand with the left hand.

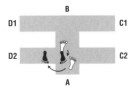

17 Keeping the same stance, execute a right punch to the palm of the left hand.

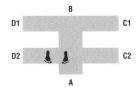

18 Cross the right foot over the left foot and execute a side kick with the left foot. Drop into a right forward stance while executing a spear finger lower thrust with the left hand by attacking the groin area with an upward palm.

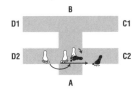

19 Move the right foot back into a right walking stance while executing a low block with the right hand.

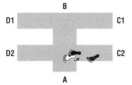

20 Move the left foot forward into a left walking stance while executing a palm block with the left hand. Pivoting on the left foot, move the right foot forward into a horse stance while executing a right elbow strike.

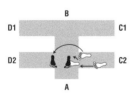

21 Keeping the same stance, execute a middle section outer block knife-hand with the right hand.

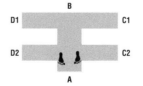

22 Keeping the same stance, execute a left punch to the palm of the right hand.

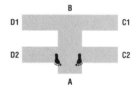

23 Cross the left foot over the right foot and execute a side kick with the right foot. Drop into a left forward stance while executing a spear finger upper thrust with the right hand by attacking the groin area with an upward palm.

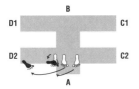

24 Move the left foot back into a left walking stance while executing a low block with the left hand.

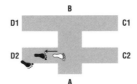

25 Move the right foot forward into a right walking stance while executing a palm block with the right hand. Pivoting on the right foot, move the left foot into a horse stance while executing a left elbow strike.

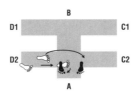

26 Keeping the right foot fixed, move the left foot inward into a ready stance. Raise both hands above the head and, moving in a circular motion, bring them down in front of the abdomen with a left-handed fist against an opened right-hand palm.

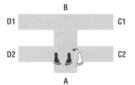

27 Pivoting on the ball of the right foot, turn to the left (180° toward B) by moving the left foot into a left forward stance while executing an outer knife-hand strike followed by a low section knife-hand strike with the left hand.

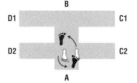

FRONT VIEW

FRONT VIEW

28 Move the right foot into right forward stance while executing a knife-hand strike to the neck followed by a low section knife-hand block with the right hand.

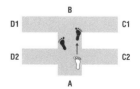

FRONT VIEW

FRONT VIEW

FRONT VIEW

29 Move the left foot into a left forward stance while executing a knife-hand strike to the neck followed by a low section knife-hand with the left hand.

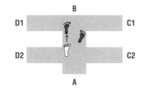

FRONT VIEW

30 Move the right foot into a right forward stance while executing an arc-hand (choking) strike to the neck with the right hand. Yell. Pivoting on the right foot, turn left (180° facing A) and return to original position with your hands in front of your face, forming a triangle.

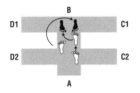

FRONT VIEW

Diamond (*Keumgan*)

Keumgan, which is compared to a diamond, originally meant "too strong to be broken." In Buddhism, *Keumgan* means "a strong combination of wisdom and virtue to break any agony of the mind." Accordingly, in Taekwondo, *Keumgan* means "movement based on spiritual strength that is as beautiful and ma-jestic as the Diamond Mountains in Korea and as hard as the diamond."

The basic practicing lines of the form correspond to the Chinese character for mountain. Therefore, a sharp and endlessly changeable majestic spirit, as that of the mountains, should be displayed.

Line and Direction of Movement

Diamond Form *(Keumgan Poomse)*

1 Starting in the ready position on the center of the line (D-C at point B, facing A), move the left foot into a left forward stance and execute a middle section inner wedge block.

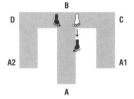

2 Move the right foot one step forward into a right forward stance and execute a right palm strike to the jaw.

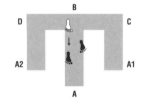

3 Move the left foot into a left forward stance and execute a left palm strike to the jaw.

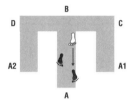

4 Move the right foot into a right forward stance and execute a right palm strike to the jaw.

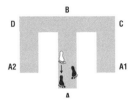

5 With the left foot fixed, move the right foot into a right back stance and execute an inside middle section knife-hand block with the left hand.

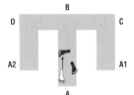

6 With the right foot fixed, move the left foot into a left back stance and execute an inside middle section knife-hand block with the left hand.

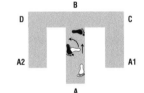

7 With the left foot fixed, move the right foot into a right back stance and execute a middle section knife-hand block with the left hand.

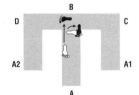

8 With the right foot fixed, lift the left foot into a right crane stance. Slowly but forcefully use the right wrist for a high section block and the left wrist for the low section (diamond block).

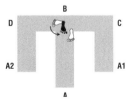

10 Pivoting on the ball of the left foot, turn to the left (360° facing A) into a horse stance while executing a left large hinge shape.

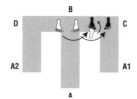

9 With the right foot fixed, put the left foot down into a horse stance and execute a left large hinge shape.

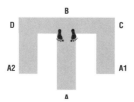

11 Lift your right foot off the ground and turn the body to the right (90° facing A1). Stomp the right foot to the ground into a powerful horse stance. Swiftly execute a mountain shape block.

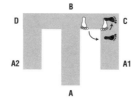

12 Pivoting on the ball of the right foot, turn to the left (180° facing D) by moving the left foot into a horse stance. Execute a middle section wedge block.

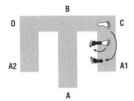

13 Keeping both feet parallel, bring both fists slightly apart from the body with palms facing inward (ease stance). Execute a slow but forceful low section wedge block.

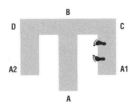

14 Pivoting on the ball of the right foot, turn the body to the right (180° facing C) and return the left foot into a powerful horse stance. Execute a mountain shape block.

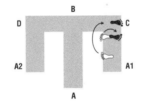

15 Pivoting on the ball of the left foot, turn the body to the right (90° facing A) while lifting the right foot into a crane stance. Slowly but forcefully use the left wrist for a high section block and the right wrist for the low section (diamond block).

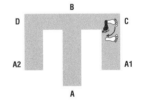

16 With the left foot fixed, put the right foot down into a horse stance and execute a right large hinge shape.

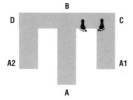

17 Pivoting on the ball of the right foot, turn the body to the right (360° facing D) into a horse stance and execute the right hinge shape.

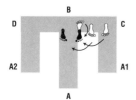

18 With the left foot fixed, lift up the right foot into a crane stance. Powerfully use the left wrist for a high section block and the right wrist for a low section side block (diamond block).

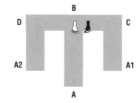

19 With the left foot fixed, return the right foot down into a horse stance and execute a right large hinge shape.

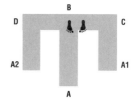

20 Pivoting on the ball of the right foot, turn the body to the right (360° facing D) into a horse stance and execute a right large hinge shape.

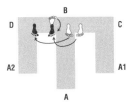

23 Keeping both feet parallel, bring both fists slightly apart from the body with palms facing inward (ease stance). Execute a slow but forceful low section wedge block.

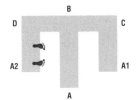

21 Pivoting on the ball of the right foot, turn the body to the left (90° facing A2) and lift the left foot into a horse stance while executing a mountain shape block.

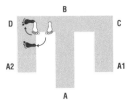

22 Pivoting on the ball of the left foot (180° facing C), turn the body to the left into a horse stance and execute a middle section inner wedge block.

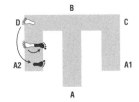

24 Pivoting on the ball of the left foot, turn the body to the left (180° facing B) into a horse stance and execute a mountain shape block.

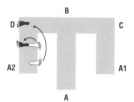

25 Pivoting on the ball of the right foot, turn the body to the left (90° facing A) while lifting the left foot up into a right crane stance. Slowly and forcefully use the right wrist for the high section block and the left wrist for a low section side block (diamond block).

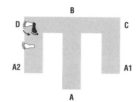

26 With the right foot fixed, return the left foot down into a horse stance and execute the left large hinge shape.

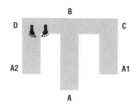

27 Pivoting on the ball of the left foot, turn the body to the left (360° facing C) into a horse stance and execute a left large hinge shape. Move the left foot back into a ready stance.

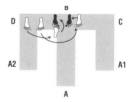

Taebaek

There is no one English word that can accurately translate the meaning of *Taebaek*. It means "light" and "looked upon as sacred." *Taebaek*, according to a Korean legend, was the place where Dangoon (the founder's name) founded the Korean nation. Today, this place is called Mount Baekdoo. Baekdoo is the loftiest and grandest mountain in Korea, and it is regarded as a symbol of Korea. Therefore, the *Taebaek* form has its basic principal movement from *Taebaek* by encompassing light, sacredness, determined will, and rigor. It is a display of grandeur.

Line and Direction of Movement

TAEBAEK

1 Starting in the ready position on the center of the line (D1-C1 at point B, facing A), pivot on the ball of the right foot and turn to the left (90° facing C1). Move the left foot into a left tiger stance and execute a low section knife-hand wedge block with the right hand.

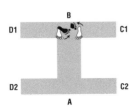

2 With the left foot fixed, execute a right front snap kick. Drop into a right forward stance and execute a middle section double punch starting with the right fist.

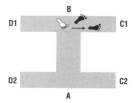

3 Pivoting on the ball of the left foot, turn to the right (180° facing D1) into a right tiger stance and execute a low section knife-hand wedge block with the left hand.

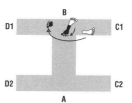

4 With the right foot fixed, execute a high section front snap kick with the left foot. Drop into a left forward stance and execute a middle section double punch starting with the left fist.

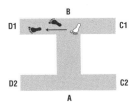

5 Pivoting on the ball of the right foot, turn to the left (90° facing A) into a left forward stance and execute a high section knife-hand strike with the right hand and a high section knife-hand block with the left hand (swallow shape knife-hand neck strike).

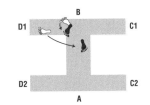

6 With the left foot fixed, move the right foot into a right forward stance while bringing the right hand down in a scooping motion. Then execute a middle section middle punch with the left fist.

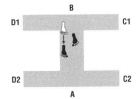

7 With the right foot fixed, move the left hand down in a scooping motion. Then move the left foot into a left forward stance and execute a middle section punch with the right fist.

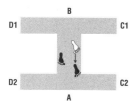

8 With the left foot fixed, move the right hand down in a scooping motion. Then move the right foot into a right forward stance and execute a middle section punch with the left fist.

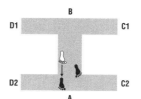

9 Pivoting on the ball of the right foot, turn the body to the left (270° facing D2) by moving the left foot into a right back stance. Slowly and forcefully use the right wrist for the high section block and the left wrist for a low section side block (diamond block).

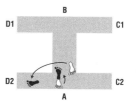

10 Keeping the same stance, move the left fist to the right shoulder and execute a right uppercut punch.

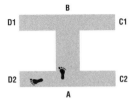

11 Remain in the same stance and execute a middle section side punch with the left fist.

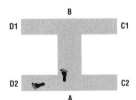

12 With the right foot fixed, lift up the left foot into a right crane stance and execute a right small hinge shape.

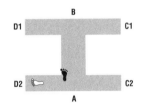

13 Simultaneously execute a left side kick and a middle section side punch with the left fist. Drop into a left forward stance and execute a right elbow strike.

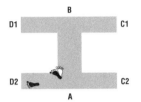

14 Move the left foot toward the right foot and then slide the right foot into a left back stance (90° facing C2). Execute a middle section diamond block.

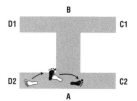

15 Remaining in the same stance, move the right fist to the left shoulder and execute a left uppercut punch.

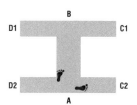

16 Remaining in the same stance, execute a side punch with the right fist.

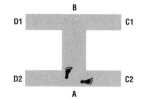

17 With the left foot fixed, lift up the right foot into a left crane stance and execute a left small hinge shape.

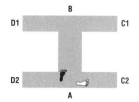

18 Simultaneously execute a right side kick and a middle section side punch with the right hand. Drop into a right forward stance and execute a left elbow strike.

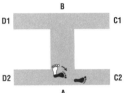

19 Move the right foot toward the left foot and slide the left foot (90° facing B) into a right back stance. Execute a middle section double knife-hand block with the left hand.

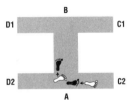

FRONT VIEW

20 With the left foot fixed, move the right foot forward into a right forward stance and execute a middle section fingertip strike with the right hand.

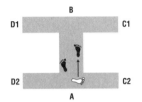

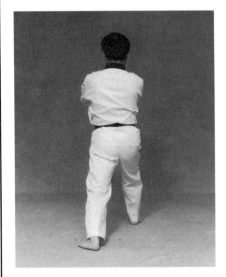

FRONT VIEW

21 Pivoting on the ball of the right foot, twist the body to the left while placing the right arm behind your back. Then move the left foot into a right back stance and execute a high section back fist with the left hand.

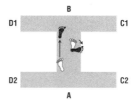

22 Move the right foot into a right forward stance and execute a middle section punch with the right fist. Yell.

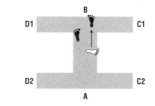

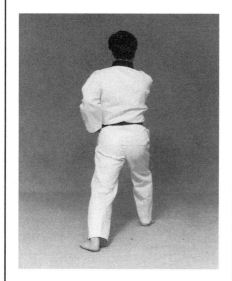

FRONT VIEW

23 Pivoting on the ball of the right foot, turn to the left (270° facing C1) by moving the left foot into a left forward stance. Execute a scissors block by using the right wrist to block the middle section and the left wrist to block the low section.

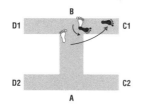

24 Execute a high section front snap kick with the right foot. Drop into a right forward stance and execute a middle section double punch starting with the right fist.

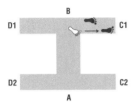

25 Pivoting on the ball of the left foot, turn to the right (180° facing D1) by moving the right foot into a right forward stance while executing the scissors block by using the right wrist to block the low section and the left wrist to block the middle section.

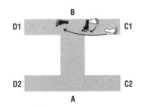

26 Execute a high section front snap kick with the left foot. Drop into a left forward stance and execute a middle section double punch starting with the left fist. Pivoting on the right foot, turn to the left (90° facing A) and move the left foot into a ready position.

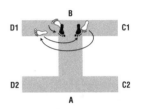

Plain *(Pyongwon)*

This form primarily applies *Koa-Seogi* (cross stance) and *Keumgang-Makki* (wrist diamond block) against the plain. The core of this form is found in the potential strength and adaptability as well as in the majestic spirit of the vast plain. The plain is where human beings live. It represents openness and grandeur where human life has lived and thrived through the abundance of food from the fertile land. Accordingly, the movement of Taekwondo represents the application of the providence of the plain, which is blessed with abundance and grace as well as vast boundlessness.

Line and Direction of Movement

1 Assume a closed stance (on the center of line D-C at point B facing A) with the left palm over the top of the right hand in front of the abdomen. Move the right foot into a ready stance while executing a low section knife-hand wedge block with both hands. Move the knife-hand slowly to the side while exhaling.

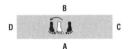

2 Keeping both feet fixed, move both hands upward to chin level, forming a triangle. Then forcefully push both hands about 1 foot forward at the neck level (push boulder).

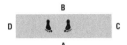

3 With the left foot fixed, move the right foot into a left back stance (90° facing D) and execute a low section knife-hand with the right hand.

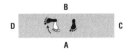

4 Turn the body to the left (180° facing C) by pivoting on your heels and moving the left foot into a right back stance. Execute a middle section knife-hand with the left hand.

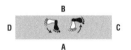

5 Slide the left foot into a forward stance and execute a right elbow jaw strike.

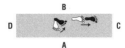

6 Execute a front snap kick with the right foot. As you land, execute a back spinning side kick with the left foot (360° counterclockwise). Assume a left back stance (facing D) and execute a middle section double knife-hand block with the right hand.

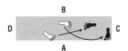

7 Keeping both feet fixed, lift the hands in a circular motion over the head and then execute a low section knife-hand block with the right hand.

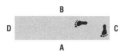

8 Move the right foot into a horse stance and then execute a double outward middle block with the right hand.

9 With the left foot fixed, lift the right foot and return to a horse stance. Pull the left fist toward the body (under the right elbow with palm downward) and then execute a back fist jaw strike with the right hand.

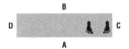

10 Staying in a horse stance, pull the right fist toward the body (under the left elbow with palm downward) and execute a back fist jaw strike with the left hand.

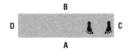

11 With the right foot fixed, move the left foot behind the right foot into a cross stance. Then execute a double elbow strike.

12 Move the right foot one step to the right into a horse stance and execute the mountain shape block.

13 With the left foot fixed, lift up the right foot into the left crane stance. Use the left wrist for a high section block and the right wrist for a low section side block (diamond block).

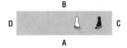

14 Remaining in the left crane stance, move both fists to the left hip area with the left hand, palm up, by the hip and the right hand, palm down, above the hip. Execute the left small hinge shape.

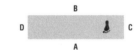

15 With the left foot fixed, execute a right side kick. Land in a right forward stance and execute a left elbow strike to the jaw.

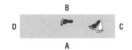

16 Execute a front snap kick with the left foot As you land, execute a back spinning side kick with the right foot (360° clockwise). Assuming a right back stance (facing C), execute a middle section double knife-hand block with the left hand.

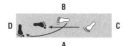

17 Keeping the same stance, lift both hands in a circular motion over the head and then execute a low section double knife-hand block with the left hand.

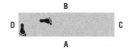

18 Move the left foot slightly out into a horse stance and execute a double outward middle block with the left hand.

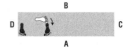

19 With the right foot fixed, lift the left foot and step down into a powerful horse stance. Pull the right fist to the body (under the left elbow with palm downward) and execute a back fist strike to the jaw with the left hand.

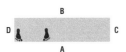

20 Staying in the horse stance, pull the left fist to the body (under the right elbow with palm downward) and execute a back fist strike to the jaw with the right fist.

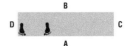

21 With the left foot fixed, place the right foot over the left foot into cross stance and then execute a double elbow strike.

22 With the right foot fixed, move the left foot one step to the side into a horse stance and execute the mountain shape block.

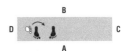

23 With the right foot fixed, lift up the left foot into a right crane stance. Use the right wrist for a high section block and the left wrist for a low section side block.

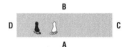

24 Keeping the same stance, execute a right small hinge shape. Then move the fists to the right hip area so that the right fist, palm up, is at the hip and the left fist, palm down, is above the hip.

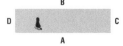

25 With the right foot fixed, execute a left side kick. Land into a left forward stance and execute a right elbow strike. Pivoting on the left foot, move the right foot to the left foot into a close stance (feet together). Place your left hand over the right hand in front of the abdomen.

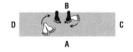

Decimal *(Sipjin)*

The term "decimal" means the number 10. In Chinese philosophy, 10 stands for endless development and growth, which are always affected by a systematic and orderly rule. The life of this form lies in the supreme change and the orderly discipline of the decimal system, which is forever increasing. This form employs primarily the outside middle block of one hand in which its wrist is guarded by the knife-hand of the other *(Son-Bakat-Geodeureo-Makki)*.

Line and Direction of Movement

DECIMAL

1 Start in a ready position at the center of D-C. Move both fists from the chest level to the belt level and then faster back up above the head (bull block). Towards the end of the block, execute a mountain block.

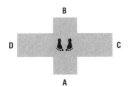

2 With the right foot fixed, move the body to the left (90° facing C) into a right back stance. Execute a middle section outer block with the left hand and use the right palm to guard the left inner wrist.

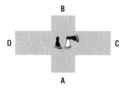

3 With the right foot fixed, move the left foot into a left forward stance. Open your left hand slowly to execute a flat fingertip strike while the right hand is held over the left elbow. Move the right hand outward and execute the flat fingertip strike.

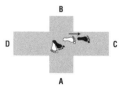

4 Keeping the same stance, execute a middle section double punch starting with the left fist.

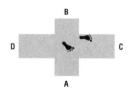

5 Pivoting on the ball of the left foot, turn the body to the right (90° facing C) by moving the right foot into a horse stance and executing a mountain shape block.

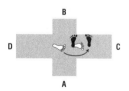

6 Keeping the right foot fixed, move the left foot to the back of the right foot into a cross stance. Then move the right foot sideways into a horse stance and execute a middle section side punch with the right fist.

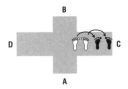

7 Pivoting on the ball of the left foot, turn to the left (180° facing D) by moving the right foot into a horse stance and executing a double elbow strike.

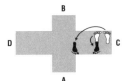

8 Bring the left foot to the right and then move the right foot into a left back stance (90° facing D). Execute a left palm guard and a right middle section outer block.

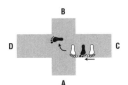

9 With the left foot fixed, move the right foot into a right forward stance. Open your right hand slowly into a flat fingertip strike while the left hand is held over the right elbow. Move the left hand outward and execute a flat fingertip strike.

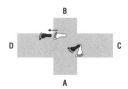

10 Keeping the same stance, execute a middle section double punch starting with the right fist.

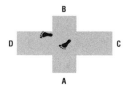

11 Pivoting on the ball of the right foot, turn the body to the right (90° facing D) by moving the left foot into a horse stance and executing a mountain shape block.

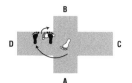

12 Keeping the left foot fixed, move the right foot behind the left foot into a cross stance. Move the left foot sideways into a horse stance and execute a middle section side punch with the left fist.

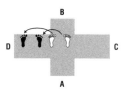

14 Bring the right foot to the right and then move the left foot into a left back stance (90° facing B). Execute a left palm guard and a middle section outer block with the right hand.

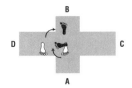

15 Move the right foot into a right forward stance. Then slowly open your right hand to execute a flat fingertip strike while the left hand is held over the right elbow. Move the left hand slowly outward to execute a flat fingertip strike.

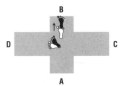

13 Pivoting on the ball of the right foot, turn to the right (180° facing A) by moving the left foot into a horse stance and executing a double elbow strike.

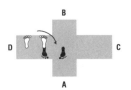

16 Remaining in the same stance, execute a middle section double punch starting with the right fist.

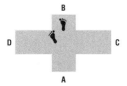

17 With the right foot fixed, move the left foot one step forward into a right back stance and execute a low section knife-hand block with the left hand.

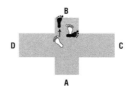

18 With the left foot fixed, move the right foot into a right forward stance. Slowly bring both hands up to form a triangle and forcefully push about a foot forward (push boulder).

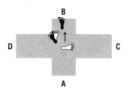

19 Shift both feet to the left (90° facing D) into a horse stance and execute middle section blocks with reverse knife-hands.

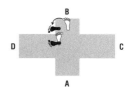

20 Remaining in the same stance, execute a low section knife-hand wedge block with both hands.

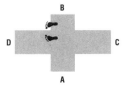

21 Keeping both feet fixed, assume a ready stance. Then slowly straighten the knees and tightly clench the fists (facing D).

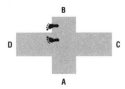

22 Pivoting on the ball of the right foot, turn left (90° facing A) by moving the left foot into a left forward stance and pulling the opponent to the chest level with the left arm (left upward scoop).

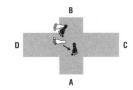

23 Keeping the same stance, bring both hands up to form a triangle and forcefully push about a foot forward (push boulder).

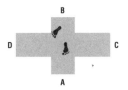

24 Execute a high section front snap kick with the right foot. Land in a right forward stance and execute two simultaneous punches, the right fist aiming at the face and the left fist aiming at the solar plexus (horizontal twin side punch).

25 Execute a high section front snap kick with the left foot. Land into a left forward stance and execute two simultaneous punches, the left fist aiming at the face and the right fist aiming at the solar plexus (horizontal twin side punch).

26 Bring both fists to the left side of the body and execute a high section front snap kick with the right foot. Spring forward so that the left foot lands behind the right foot in a cross stance. Then execute the right back guarding face strike.

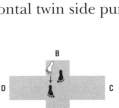

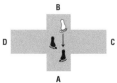

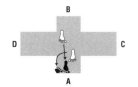

27 Pivoting on the ball of the right foot, turn the body to the left (180° facing B) by moving the left foot into a left forward. Bring both hands up to form a triangle and push about a foot forward (push boulder).

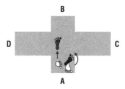

28 With the right foot fixed, move the left foot back into a forward horse stance and execute the low section knife-hand cross block.

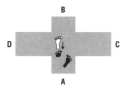

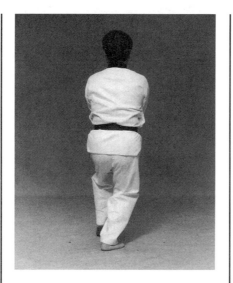

29 With the left foot fixed, move the right foot one step forward into a left back stance and execute a middle section reverse knife-hand block with the right hand.

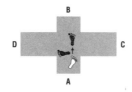

FRONT VIEW

30 With the right foot fixed, move the left foot one step forward into a right back stance and execute two simultaneous punches, the left fist aiming at the face and the right fist aiming at the solar plexus (horizontal twin side punch).

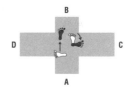

31 With the left foot fixed, move the right foot one step forward into a left back stance and execute two simultaneous punches, the right fist aiming at the face and the left fist aiming at the solar plexus (horizontal twin side punch). Pivoting on the ball of the right foot, turn the body to the right (180° facing A) by moving the left foot into a ready stance.

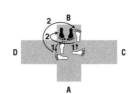

Earth (*Jitae*)

According to Eastern belief, all living things come from and return to the earth. The earth is the origin and the termination of life. This form applies to movements that are derived from the harmony of a strong mind and strong muscles—just as the universal mind of the earth lies implicitly in the vigor of life.

EARTH

1 Start in a ready position at the center of D-C. Turn to the left (90° facing C) by moving the left foot into a left back stance while executing an outer block with the left arm.

2 Slowly move the right foot into a right forward stance, and slowly but forcefully execute a high block with the right hand followed by a middle section punch with the left fist.

3 Pivoting on the ball of the left foot, turn to the right (180° facing D) by moving the right foot into a left back stance. Simultaneously execute an outer block with the right arm.

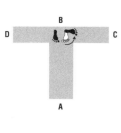

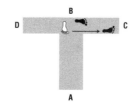

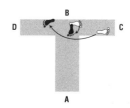

4 Slowly move the left foot slowly into a left forward stance, and slowly but forcefully execute a high block with the left hand, followed by a middle section punch with the right punch.

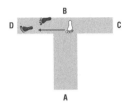

5 Pivoting on the ball of the right foot, turn to the left (90° facing A) by moving the left foot into a left forward stance and executing a low block with the left arm.

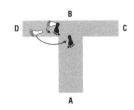

6 With the right foot fixed, bring the left foot slightly back into a right back stance. Then execute a high section knife-hand with the left hand.

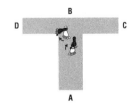

7 With the left foot fixed, execute a high section front snap kick with the right foot. Land in a left back stance and execute a low section knife-hand with the right hand.

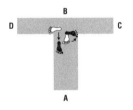

9 With the right foot fixed, execute a high section left front snap kick with the left foot. Land in a right back stance and execute a low section knife-hand with the left hand.

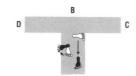

10 Move the left foot into a left forward stance and execute a high block with the left hand.

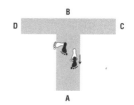

8 Staying in the same stance, slowly but forcefully execute a middle outward block with the right hand.

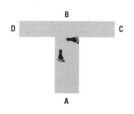

11 Move the right foot into a right forward stance and execute a simultaneous high block with the left arm and front punch with the right fist (diamond shape front punch).

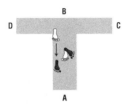

12 Keeping the same stance, execute a inward middle block with the left hand followed immediately by an inward middle block with the right hand.

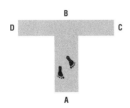

13 With the left foot fixed, move the right foot back into a right back stance and execute a low section knife-hand with the left hand.

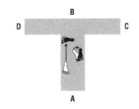

14 With the left foot fixed, execute a high section front snap kick with the right foot and return to its original position. Slide the left foot into a left forward stance and execute a middle section double punch starting with the right fist.

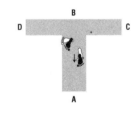

Still in the horse stance, execute a middle section knife-hand outer block with the right hand (facing A).

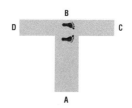

16 Keeping the same stance, execute a low block with the left arm (facing B).

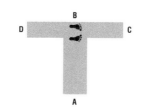

15 Pivoting on the ball of the right foot, turn to the left (90° facing C) by moving the left foot into a horse stance. Bring both fists up from waist level, increasing your speed as you go above the head (bull block).

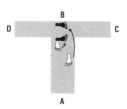

18 Still in the horse stance, execute a hammer fist strike with the left hand (facing A) in the palm of the right hand. Yell.

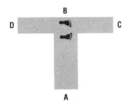

19 With the left foot fixed, lift up the right foot into a left crane stance and execute a low block with the right hand.

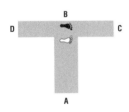

20 Still in the left crane stance, move both fists to the left hip and execute the small hinge shape.

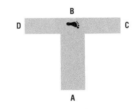

21 Execute a high section side kick with the right foot. Land where the left foot is and assume a right crane stance. Execute a low block with the left hand (facing B).

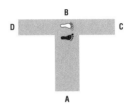

22 Keeping the same stance, move both fists to the right hip and execute the right small hinge shape.

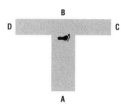

23 With the right foot fixed, execute a middle section side kick with the left foot. Land in a left forward stance and execute a middle section punch with the right fist.

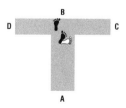

24 With the left foot fixed, move the right foot into a right forward stance and execute a middle section straight punch with the right fist. Keep the fist in line with the right leg.

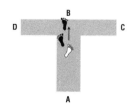

25 Pivoting on the ball of the right foot, turn to the left (270° facing C) by moving the left foot into a right back stance and executing a low section knife-hand block with the left hand.

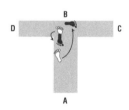

26 With the left foot fixed, move the right foot one step forward into a left back stance and execute a middle section knife-hand block with the right hand.

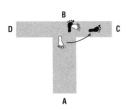

27 Pivoting on the ball of the left foot, turn to the right (180° facing D) by moving the right foot into a left back stance and executing a low section knife-hand block with the right hand.

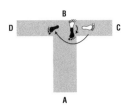

28 With the right foot fixed, move the left foot one step forward into a right back stance and execute a middle section knife-hand block with the left hand. With the right foot fixed, turn to the left (90° facing A), into the original position.

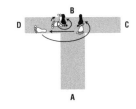

Sky *(Cheonkwon)*

To the limited mind, the sky is infinitely vast, mysterious, and filled with wonder. From ancient times, Asians have worshipped the sky as the ruler of the universe and the controller of all things in nature. The sky form is composed of motions that are full of piety and vitality. It is as if a man is looking to the sky with open arms and imagining himself as an eagle soaring through it.

Line and Direction of Movement

SKY

1 Stand with your feet together (closed stance) at point B. Keep your hands open at the abdomen level with the left hand over the right hand. Bring both hands up to the chest level while inhaling.

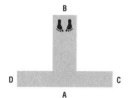

2 Push both hands out toward the sides at shoulder level with the palms pointing outward. Close them in front of your chest, left hand in front of right hand, and then bring them overhead. The arm motion should be like an eagle spreading its wings.

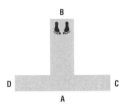

3 Bring both hands up in front of the chest, then move the left foot one step backward into a right tiger stance while simultaneously executing a double knuckle fist spring strike (hitting with the knuckles of the middle finger).

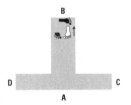

4 Pivoting slightly on the balls of both feet, twist the body to the right into a right forward stance and execute an outward middle section knife-hand block with the left hand.

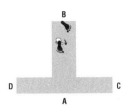

5 Pull the left hand to the left hip and move the left foot into a left forward stance. Then execute a middle section punch with the right fist.

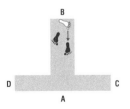

8 Keeping the same stance, turn your upper body slightly to the right and execute a middle section knife-hand outer block with the left hand.

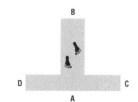

6 Keeping the same stance, turn your upper body slightly to the left and execute an outward middle section knife-hand block with the right hand.

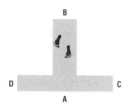

7 Bring the right hand to the right hip and move the right foot into a right forward stance. Then execute a middle section punch with the left fist.

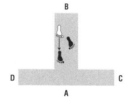

...th the right foot ...ed, pull the left hand ...st to the chest and execute a side kick with the left foot. Yell. Drop the left foot into a left forward stance and execute a low section block with the left arm.

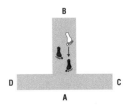

10 Move the right foot into a right forward stance and execute a middle section straight punch with the right fist. Keep the fist in line with the right leg.

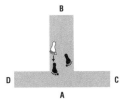

11 Pivoting on the ball of the right foot, turn to the right (270° facing D) by moving the left foot into a right back stance and executing a double outward middle block with the left arm.

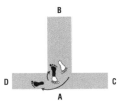

12 Keeping the same stance, move the left wrist in a circular motion toward the outside and execute a middle section side punch with the left fist.

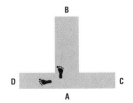

15 Keeping the left back stance, move the right wrist outward in a circular motion and then execute a side punch with the right fist.

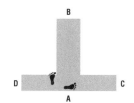

13 Move the right foot one step forward into a left back stance (facing D) and execute a high section outer block with the left hand, followed by a middle section side punch with the right fist.

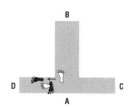

14 Pivoting on the ball of the left foot, turn to the right (180° facing C) by moving the right foot into a left back stance and execute a double outward middle block with the right arm.

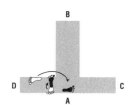

16 Move the left foot one step forward into a right back stance and execute a high section outer block with the right hand, following immediately with a side punch with the left fist.

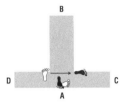

17 Pivoting on the ball of the right foot, turn the body to the left (90° facing B) by moving the left foot into a left forward stance and executing an outward middle block with the right hand.

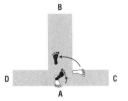

FRONT VIEW

18 Keeping the same stance, execute a middle section punch with the left fist. Keep the fist in line with the left leg.

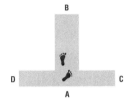

19 With the left foot fixed, execute a high section front snap kick with the right foot. Land in a right forward stance and execute a middle section punch with the right fist. Keep the fist in line with the right leg.

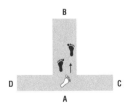

while the right wrist touches the left palm. Then execute a right low section block.

FRONT VIEW

20 With the left foot fixed, move the right foot slightly back into a left back stance and execute a low section knife-hand block with the right hand.

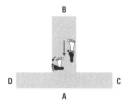

21 Quickly slide forward a half step while the left palm touches the right wrist. Then execute an outward middle block with the right hand. Immediately take another half step,

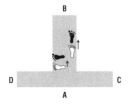

FRONT VIEW

22 With the left foot fixed, move the right foot to the left (90° facing D) into a horse stance and execute a simultaneous high block with the left arm and side punch with the right fist (diamond shape side punch).

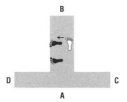

SIDE VIEW

23 Jumping off the right foot, spin left (360° facing B) and execute an inside crescent kick before your feet touch the ground. Land into a horse stance and execute a diamond block (left wrist in a high section block and right wrist in a middle section block).

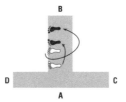

SIDE VIEW

FRONT VIEW

24 With the right foot fixed, turn the body to the left (facing A) by moving the left foot into a right back stance. Execute a low section knife-hand block with the left hand and a high section outer block with the right hand.

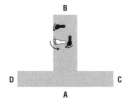

25 Turn the body to the right (facing B) into a left back stance. Execute a low section knife-hand block with the right hand and a high section outer knife-block with the left hand (facing B).

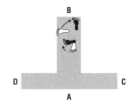

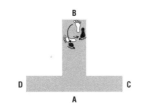

26 Pivoting on the ball of the right foot, turn the body to the left (180° facing A) and bring both feet together. Open both hands from the waist and bring them upward in a circular motion. Move the right foot one step forward into a right tiger stance while slowly but forcefully executing a push mountain shape block.

27 Move forward the left foot together with the right foot. Open both hands from the waist and bring them upward in a circular motion. Then move the left foot one step forward into a left tiger stance while slowly but forcefully executing a push mountain shape block. Move forward the left foot together with the right foot. Bring both opened hands in front of the abdomen with the left hand over the right.

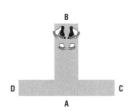

Water (*Hansoo*)

The water is seen as the source of life and origin of all things in the universe. From one drop of this precious natural fluid, rivers and then oceans were formed. Although water can be serene and calm, it can also be wild and furious. These qualities, in addition to water's fluidity and adaptability, are projected in Taekwondo movements. Therefore, the beautiful and coordinated movements of this form can also be as forceful as water.

WATER

1 Stand in a closed stance (at point E facing A) with opened hands, the left hand in front of the right, at the abdomen level. Move the left foot into a left forward stance and execute middle section blocks with reverse knife-hands.

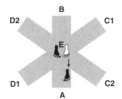

2 Move the right foot into a right forward stance and execute a double hammer fist strike to the ribs.

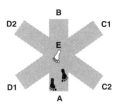

3 With the left foot fixed, move the right foot one step back into a right forward stance (towards B) while executing a mountain shape block.

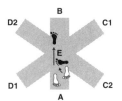

4 Keeping both feet fixed, turn the body to the left into a left forward stance while executing a middle section straight punch with the right fist.

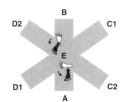

5 With the right foot fixed, move the left foot back into a left back stance (towards B) while executing a mountain shape block.

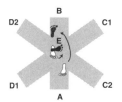

6 Keeping both feet fixed, turn the body to the right into a right forward stance while executing a middle section straight punch with the left hand.

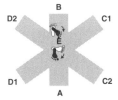

7 With the left foot fixed, move the right foot back into a right forward stance (towards B) while executing a mountain shape block.

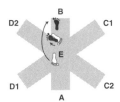

8 Keeping both feet fixed, turn the body to the left into a left forward stance while executing a middle section straight punch with the right fist.

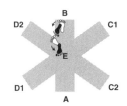

9 With the left foot fixed, move the right foot into a right forward stance while executing middle section blocks with reverse knife-hands.

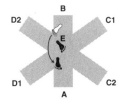

10 With the right foot fixed, move the left foot to the left (45° facing C2) into a left forward stance while executing a left arc hand (choking) strike to the neck.

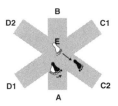

12 With the right foot fixed, move the left foot one step back into a horse stance (facing C1). Execute a low section inner wrist block with the right hand while grabbing the opponent with the other hand.

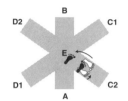

11 Quickly move the right foot forward into a close stance. Then execute a double fisted upper punch.

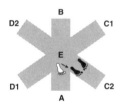

14 With the right foot fixed, turn the body to the left (90° facing C1) while lifting the left foot into a right crane stance. Execute a right small hinge shape and then bring both fists to the right hip area.

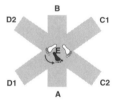

13 Pivoting on the left foot, turn the body to the right (facing A) by moving the right foot one step back into a right back stance while using the right wrist for a high section block and the left wrist for a low section block (diamond block).

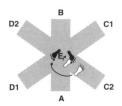

15 With the right foot fixed, execute a high section side kick with the left foot. Land into a left forward stance while executing a high section knife-hand strike with the right hand and a high section knife-hand block with the left hand (swallow shape knife-hand neck strike).

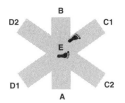

16 Execute a high section front snap kick with the right foot and jump forward so that you land in a right forward cross stance (facing C1) while executing a high section back fist with the right hand. Yell.

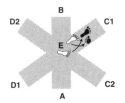

17 With the right foot fixed, move the left foot out into a horse stance (facing B) while executing an outer knife-hand strike with the left hand.

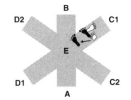

18 Pivoting on the ball of the left foot, execute an inner crescent kick with the right foot to the palm of the left hand. Land in a horse stance (facing C2) while executing a right elbow strike to the palm of the left hand.

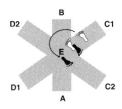

21 Pivoting on the ball of the left foot, move the right foot one step back into a horse stance (facing D2) while executing a low section inner wrist target block with the left hand.

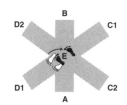

19 Move the left foot toward the right foot, then move the right foot into a right forward stance (facing D1) while executing a right arc hand (choking) strike to the neck.

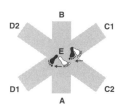

20 Bring the left foot forward into a close stance while executing a double fisted upper punch.

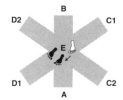

22 Pivoting on the right foot, turn the body to the left while moving the left foot one step back into a left back stance (facing D1) while using the left wrist for a high section block and the right wrist for a low section block (diamond block).

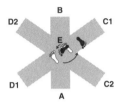

23 With the left foot fixed, turn the body to the right (90° facing D2) while lifting the right foot into the left crane stance. Execute a left small hinge shape and then bring both fists to the left hip area.

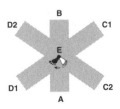

24 With the left foot fixed, execute a high section side kick with the right foot. Land in a right forward stance while executing a swallow shape knife-hand neck strike with the left hand.

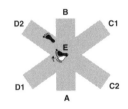

25 Execute a high section front snap kick with the left foot and jump forward so that you land in a left cross stance while executing a high section back fist with the left hand. Yell.

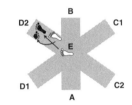

27 Pivoting on the ball of the right foot, execute an inside crescent kick with the left foot to the palm of the right hand. Land in a horse stance (facing D1) while executing a left elbow strike to the palm of the right hand. Bring the right foot toward the left foot (at point E, facing A) and assume a close stance. Bring the left hand over the right hand in front of the abdomen.

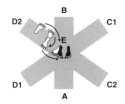

26 With the left foot fixed, move the right foot out into a horse stance (facing B) and then execute an outward knife-hand strike with the right hand.

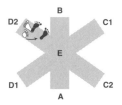

Oneness *(Ilyo)*

Oneness is the state of spiritual cultivation in which the mind and body, the spirit and matter, are unified. It is a state of pure mind from profound faith in which all worldly desires are discarded. In this state, the ego is overcome and the ultimate ideal of Taekwondo is achieved. The final goal pursued in Taekwondo is a discipline in which concentration is in every movement so that all worldly thoughts and obsessions are shaken off.

ONENESS

1 Beginning a closed stance (at point B, facing A1), bring both hands up to your face with the left hand cupping over the right fist. With the right foot fixed, move the left foot one step forward into a right back stance while executing a high section knife-hand block with the left hand.

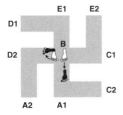

2 With the left foot fixed, move the right foot into a right forward stance and execute a middle section straight punch with the right fist.

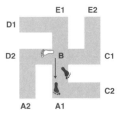

3 With the right foot fixed, move the left foot slowly but firmly toward the left (90° facing C2) into a right back stance while using the right wrist for a high section block and the left wrist for a low section block (diamond block).

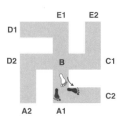

4 Pivoting on the ball of the right foot, turn the body to the left (90° facing E1) by moving the left foot into a right back stance while executing a middle section knife-hand block with the left hand.

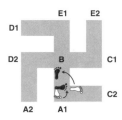

5 Remaining in the same stance, execute a middle section punch with the right fist.

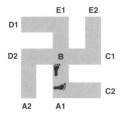

6 Move the right foot one step forward and bring the left foot behind the right knee into a right crane back stance. Then execute a right fingertip strike. Yell.

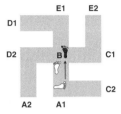

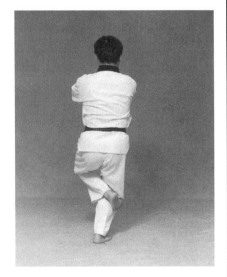

7 With the right foot fixed, slowly and firmly execute a simultaneous mountain shape block and left side kick (facing E1).

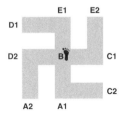

8 Land into a right back stance while executing a high X block.

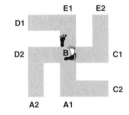

9 With the left foot fixed, slowly yet firmly move the right foot into a right forward stance while executing a middle section straight punch with the right fist.

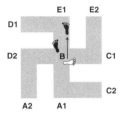

10 With the right foot fixed, slowly and firmly move the left foot one step toward the left (90° facing D1) into a right back stance. Use the right wrist for a high section block and the left wrist for a low section block (diamond block).

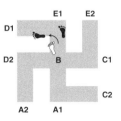

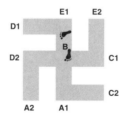

12 Keeping the same stance, execute a middle section straight punch with the right fist.

11 Pivoting on the ball of the right foot, turn the body to the left (90° facing A1) by moving the left foot into a right back stance. Then execute a middle section double knife-hand block.

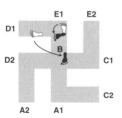

14 With the right foot fixed, slowly execute a simultaneous mountain shape block and left side kick (facing C1).

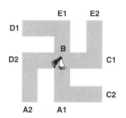

13 Quickly and power fully move the right foot one step forward and bring the left foot behind the right knee (right crane back stance). Then execute a fingertip strike with the right hand. Yell.

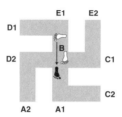

15 Land in a right back stance while executing a high X block.

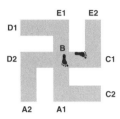

16 With the left foot fixed, move the right foot in a right forward stance. Open both hands and then twist and pull them inward to your waist. Execute a middle section straight punch with the right fist.

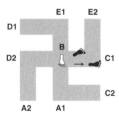

17 Move the left foot to the left (90° facing E2) into a right back stance while slowly and firmly using the right wrist for a high section block and the left wrist for a low section block (diamond block).

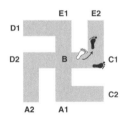

18 Pivoting on the ball of the right foot, turn the body to the left (90°facing D2) by moving the left foot slowly into a close stance while bringing your fists to your waist.

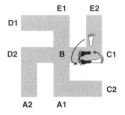

19 Execute a high section front snap kick with the right foot. As you land, immediately execute a left jump side kick landing with the right foot and land in a right back stance while executing a high X block.

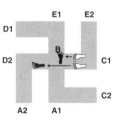

20 With the left foot fixed, move the right foot into a right forward stance. Open both hands, and then twist and pull them inward to your waist. Execute a middle section straight punch with the right fist.

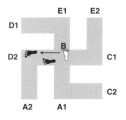

21 Pivoting on the ball of the left foot, turn the body to the left (90° facing A2) by moving the right foot into a right back stance while slowly and firmly using the right wrist for a high section block and the left wrist for a low section block (diamond block).

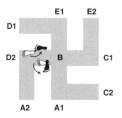

22 With the right foot fixed, turn the body to the left (90° facing C1) while bringing the right foot into a close stance. Bring both fists to the waist.

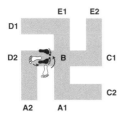

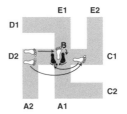

23 Execute a high section front snap kick with the left foot. As you land, immediately execute a right jump side kick and land into a left back stance while executing a high X block. With the left foot fixed, move the right foot back to a close stance (facing A1). Bring both hands up to your face with the left hand cupping over the right fist.

7

Breaking

Breaking is a demonstration of the power and control that the student achieves through the study of martial arts. It is the ability to focus and direct one's mental power, positive energy, and physical strength toward a specific point on a target in order to break it. Although it is not the main goal of the art, breaking is still one of its most interesting, exciting, and spectacular aspects.

In Taekwondo, the student's status is shown by the color of the belt worn. At each belt level, the student achieves better mental and physical power, concentration, and relaxation, which can be precisely directed to a target.

When the student starts, he holds a white belt to indicate that he is a beginner. The student progresses to the yellow belt, then to orange, green, purple, blue, red, brown, red/black, and finally the black belt—the highest-color belt. As a black belt, the student has mastered all the basics of the art and is on his way to learn the highest and the most advanced techniques in Taekwondo.

The black belt level progresses from the 1st to 9th degree in Taekwondo. Achieving the highest levels takes years of hard work, persistence, and training under well-qualified masters. As a student progresses in his belt levels and degrees, he gradually increases in physical strength, mental power, self-confidence, and self-control. He also increases his ability to relax and gain total concentration and focus—qualities necessary for the perfection of actions and successful demonstration. One visible proof of his progression is his breaking ability.

A human target obviously cannot be used to demonstrate breaking. Instead, the master and students demonstrate their power on wooden boards, bricks, rocks, cement blocks, and even sometimes cast-iron bars. Breaking helps develop and improve personal speed and power. It helps one mark one's progress as well as compares one's performance to other students. It also demonstrates to one's instructor the personal progress one has made.

In the process of breaking, the master and student combine their mental and physical forces to carry the desired blow with perfect, precise focus. Focus is the most important factor in breaking successfully without injury. This is accomplished only when the student allows his body to be completely relaxed before striking. Tension should only take place at the moment of impact (a fraction of a second). Perfect focus can only be achieved with time and practice. For this reason, choosing a qualified master to guide you in learning to break and helping you understand the steps to break properly is important. *Do not try to break anything by yourself without proper technique and supervision, or else you could easily be hurt.* With the proper guidance, however, breaking can become exhilarating and, at times, a phenomenal experience.

In addition to the mental aspects of

breaking, both posture and movement are essential. Posture includes stance (for stability and proper balance), distance (for maximum effectiveness), and striking angle (for preventing injury). Movement entails swinging the body correctly through shifting your weight and body parts in order to carry a sufficient force *through* the target. It gathers the whole body mass and adds it to the strike for a more powerful blow. The contact point is vital. For example, the contact point for a knife-hand strike is the meaty part of the hand opposite the thumb. Otherwise, striking at the wrong angle can injury the pinkie finger. In a straight punch, the strike point is the first two knuckles.

If the target is being held, the person must hold it firmly at the correct height and angle. The holder should assume a forward stance with the elbows locked in order to provide a stable target. If the target is not held properly, the force of the blow will be absorbed and the board will not break. Teamwork is important.

Here are some examples of what proper breaking can achieved:

PALM STRIKE

SPINNING BACK KICK

KNIFE-HAND STRIKE

FINGERTIP STRIKE

KNIFE-HAND STRIKE
(WITH PALM DOWN)

8
Sparring

Sparring is a practical exercise in self-defense. The student draws on all aspects of the martial art—the mental, physical, and technical—against the skill and power of an opponent. The keys to successful sparring are quick reflexes, boldness, good judgment, precise timing, a variety of techniques, intense focus on the target, correct distance, good balance, control of each movement, and persistence. In Taekwondo, sparring employs the self-defense moves learned from performing the *poomse*: basic kicks, combination kicks, blocks, punches, strikes, side steps, back steps, sliding steps, change steps, and fakes.

Sparring can be divided into three categories: practical situations, exhibitions, and competitive events. When sparring is done in a practical situation, such as a means of self-defense, it is called the technical aspect of the art, which has no rules. An unprovoked attack might become a matter of life or death. In such a situation, a good Taekwondo student will use good judgment and apply only the force necessary to get rid of the aggressor. Reasonable force will be targeted against the attacker's vital points.

Through sparring practice, the student learns to overcome his fear or panic of being in a fighting situation. This training will provide the good reflexes, concentration, speed, and self-control needed in a real confrontation. Because of discipline and self-control gained in class, the student learns to get out of

a bad situation without suffering repercussions of his actions.

In exhibition sparring, the student applies his techniques in a controlled setting by following basic rules and demonstrating reasonable restraint against his opponent, since the opponent is a theoretical, not real-life, attacker. Graceful and powerful displays of attack and counterattack demonstrate the various blocks, kicks, punches, and combination techniques. Physical prowess is combined with concentration, self-discipline, precise focus, and timing. Self-control and quick reflexes are important not only for winning but also for preventing injuries.

When sparring is done in competition, participants follow official rules and regulations for points awarded or deducted, for proper or improper attacks to the target area. Before each match, the students are reminded about the designated and prohibited target areas. They are also reminded of the time limits for the match when the final score is calculated. Good reflexes, boldness, speed, good judgment, and a sense of distance are necessary to win.

ONE-STEP SPARRING

The main purpose of one-step sparring is to expose the students to a controlled situation in which to prepare for free sparring. In this practice, students learn how to measure their distance, maintain good balance and self-control, and develop good coordination. In short, they practice self-defense with the assurance of not hurting each other.

In the following one-step sparring exercise, the student on the right will be performing the self-defense moves. Except for step 1, only her movements will be described.

1 Stand facing each other and bow. The first student (on the left) assumes a left forward stance and low left block. The second student (on the right) yells when she is ready.

2 Move the right foot into a right forward stance and execute an inside middle block with the right arm followed by a double punch to the solar plexus, starting with the left fist.

3 Move the left foot one step forward into a left back stance and execute an inside middle block with the left arm, followed by a right punch to the ribs and then a left punch to the face.

4 Move the right foot into a right forward stance. Execute a knife-hand strike to the neck with the right hand while raising the left hand with palm out in front of the head for a block (rising knife block).

5 Move the right foot into a right forward stance. Strike the neck with an inside right hand-knife while performing a high block with the left hand. Holding the opponent's wrist with the left hand, strike the neck with an outside hand knife.

6 Move the right foot forward into a back stance and execute a left knife-hand block. Grab the opponent's right wrist with the left hand and punch the solar plexus with the right fist. Using the left leg, sweep the opponent's right foot. When the opponent falls to the floor, execute a right punch to the face.

7 Move the right foot one step forward into a forward stance and execute a middle section inside block. Quickly turn around and execute an elbow strike with the left elbow.

8 Execute a left forward stance and a left low block. Punch the opponent's face.

9 Move the left foot into a left forward stance and execute a high X block. Hold the opponent's right wrist with the left hand and strike the neck with an inside hand-knife strike using the right hand. Grab the back of the neck and pull the head down as you execute a right knee strike to the solar plexus.

10 Move the left foot into a left forward stance and execute a middle section outer knife-hand with the right hand. Hold the opponent's right hand as you execute a middle section roundhouse kick with the right foot. Follow immediately with a side kick using the right leg.

11 Block with an inside crescent kick using the left foot, and then execute a high section roundhouse kick with the right foot.

Appendix

KUKKIWON:
WORLD TAEKWONDO HEADQUARTERS

The Secretariat of the World Taekwondo Federation (WTF) is located in Seoul, South Korea, in a beautiful edifice called Kukkiwon. Kukkiwon was constructed in 1971 and is distinctive for its traditional Korean style of architecture. It provides a home for international Taekwondo-related organizations and furnishes its practitioners with modern facilities for both training and competition.

The main focus at Kukkiwon is on Taekwondo as an art form. Its masters continually develop and improve kicking, striking, and defensive techniques. Its personnel conduct promotion tests and issue certificates to Taekwondo students of all the national associations that are members. Its masters train and certify instructors to spread the teachings of modern Taekwondo throughout the world. The WTF assists designers who develop protective equipment used in competition. The executives of Kukkiwon ensure that the quality of the art is protected, and they delegate any functions regarding competitive activities to the members of the WTF.

WORLD TAEKWONDO FEDERATION

The World Taekwondo Federation is the international organization representing Taekwondo as a sport. Modern Taekwondo is the only martial art with an international organization. It was officially established on May 28, 1973, at the inauguration meeting held at Kukkiwon with the participation of 35 representatives from around the world. WTF is responsible for an estimated 30 million Taekwondo practitioners in approximately 130 countries. The organization has more than 4000 Korean instructors and coaches outside of Korea helping many local instructors. It also trains masters who give regional referee seminars in order to standardize the rules of competition.

WTF has established global branches through national organizations and national unions to maintain quality instruction and competition and to reinforce its standardized rules and regulations. Anyone who competes internationally must be a member of his national organization. In the United States, the organization is called the United Taekwondo Union.

WTF'S AFFILIATION WITH INTERNATIONAL SPORTS ORGANIZATIONS

The following traces the history of the World Taekwondo Federation from 1975 through 1994.

OCTOBER 1975:	Affiliated with the General Association of International Sports Federations (GAISF).
APRIL 1976:	Adopted by the International Military Sports Council (IMSC) as its 23rd official sport.
JULY 1980:	Recognized by the International Olympic Committee (IOC).
JANUARY 1981:	Affiliated with the International Council of Sports Science & Physical Education (ICSSPE).
JULY 1981:	Participated in the World Games 1 as an official event.
AUGUST 1983:	Adopted by the Pan American Games and made its debut in 1987 Pan American Games in Indianapolis, Indiana.
OCTOBER 1983:	Affiliated with the International Group for Construction of Sports and Leisure Facilities (IAKS).
NOVEMBER 1983:	Adopted by the Supreme Council for Sports in Africa (SCSA) as an official sport of All-African Games.
SEPTEMBER 1984:	Adopted by the Olympic Council of Asia (OCA) as an official sport of the 1986 Asian Games in Seoul, Korea.
JUNE 1985:	Adopted by the Executive Board of the IOC as a demonstration sport of the 1988 Olympic Games in Seoul, Korea.
MAY 1986:	Affiliated with the Comité Internationale pour le Fair-Play.
MAY 1986:	Adopted as a Fédération Internationale du Sport Universitaire (FISU) event for the World University Championships at the FISU Executive Committee meeting held in Zagreb, Croatia.
JANUARY 1990:	Adopted by the Central American Sports Organization as an official sport of the Central American Sports Games.
AUGUST 1991:	Adopted by the Bolivian Directive Council as the regular program of the 1993 Bolivian Games in Cochabamba, Bolivia.
APRIL 1992:	Adopted by the OCA as an official sport of the Hiroshima Asian Games scheduled for October 2–6, 1994.
AUGUST 1992:	Staged in the 1992 Olympic Games in Barcelona, Spain, as a demonstration sport.
SEPTEMBER 1994:	Announcement of the inclusion of Taekwondo in the 2000 Olympics to be held in Sydney, Australia.

The rules of competition manage fairly and smoothly all matters pertaining to all levels of Taekwondo competition. The World Taekwondo Federation and the members of its national and regional associations or unions ensure the global application of these standardized rules and regulations. In order to be recognized, organized, and promoted by the World Taekwondo Federation, a Taekwondo competition must follow all of the Federation's rules and regulations. If any member of a national association wishes to modify some part of the competition rules, it must first gain the approval of the world body by submitting the contents of the desired amendment along with the reasons for the desired change. The approval of any changes in these rules must be received from the World Taekwondo Federation one month prior to the scheduled competition.

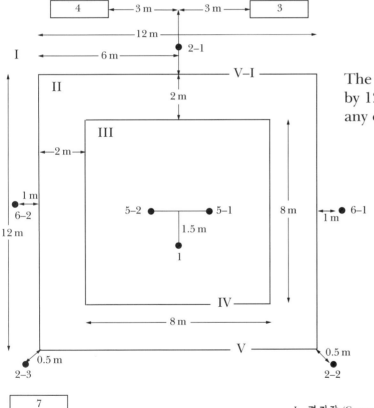

The competition area measures 12 meters by 12 meters and has a flat surface without any obstructing projections.

I 경기장 (Competition Area)

II 경계지역 (Alert Area)

III 경기지역 (Contest Area)

IV 경계선 (Alert Line)

V 한계선 (Boundary Line)

V-I 제1한계선 (1st Boundary Line)

1. 주심 위치 (Referee's Mark)
2. 부심 위치 (Judge's Mark)
3. 기록원 위치 (Recorder's Mark)
4. 임석의사 위치 (Commission Doctor's Mark)
5-1. 청선수 위치 (Blue Contestant's Mark)
5-2. 홍선수 위치 (Red Contestant's Mark)
6-1. 청선수의 코치 위치 (Blue Coach's Mark)
6-2. 홍선수의 코치 위치 (Red Coach's Mark)
7. 검사대 (Inspection Desk)

OFFICIALS' QUALIFICATIONS AND DUTIES

Referees

QUALIFICATION

International Referee certificate registered by the World Taekwondo Federation.

DUTIES

1. The referee shall maintain control over the match.
2. The referee shall declare the beginning (*shi-jak*) and end (*keuman*) of the competition, the break (*kalyeo*), and the continuing (*kyesok*). The referee shall also keep the time record (*kyeshi*), declare the winner and loser, deduct points, and administer the warning and retiring. All the referee's declarations shall be made when the results are confirmed.
3. The referee shall have the right to made decisions independently in accordance with the prescribed rules.
4. The referee shall not award points.
5. In case of a tied or scoreless match, the decision of superiority shall be made by the referee after the end of three rounds.

REQUIREMENTS FOR OFFICIATING

The referee must have a full understanding of the competition area's dimensions and have a full knowledge of how to utilize these dimensions to the full limits of the area in order to avoid excessive interruption of the match. He should remain alert at all times to be able to detect if a contestant leaves the alert area with the intent of mismanaging the game or avoiding the exchange of techniques. In this case, the referee must declare *kalyeo* and assess a penalty. He must promptly declare *kalyeo* if both feet of both contestants cross the alert line or take responsibility for any occurrence caused by his delay.

GUIDELINES FOR OFFICIATING

The judgment of the validity of techniques is related to the boundaries of the competition area and depends on the timing of the referee's declaration of *kalyeo* (break). The referee bases the declaration of *kalyeo* partially on the relative positions of the contestants to the alert line. The contestants and judges base their respective actions and decisions partially on the referee's declaration of *kalyeo*.

The referee's criterion for the declaration of *kalyeo* is the point at which one foot of either contestant crosses the alert line. To declare *kalyeo* in the absence of violations or safety considerations, or before one foot of either contestant crosses the alert line, is unusual; however, depending on the circumstances of the match, these instantaneous decisions follow the judgment of the referee.

When the referee deems it appropriate to allow the match to continue uninterrupted until that instant when both contestants have completely crossed over the alert line, he may do so and can declare *kalyeo* at his or her discretion.

Judges

QUALIFICATION

International Judge certificate registered by the World Taekwondo Federation.

DUTIES

1. The judges shall mark the valid points immediately.
2. The judges shall state their opinions forthrightly when requested to do so by the referee.

Referees and Judges

Decisions made by the referees and judges shall be conclusive, and they shall be held responsible to the Board of Arbitration for those decisions.

UNIFORMS

1. Referees and judges shall wear the uniform designated by the World Taekwondo Federation.
2. Referees and judges shall not carry or take any materials to the arena that might interfere with the contest.

Assistants

QUALIFICATION

Assistants shall be adults and have good knowledge and experience in Taekwondo.

DUTIES

1. Assistants shall time the contest and the period of time-out.
2. Assistants shall record and publicize the awarded and deducted points.

CONTESTANTS' QUALIFICATIONS

1. The participant should have the nationality of the participating team (verified by a passport).
2. The participant must be recommended by the National Taekwondo Association.
3. The participant must have a certificate of proof that his or her Taekwondo *dan* (belt) was issued by the Kukkiwon/World Taekwondo Federation. In the World Junior Taekwondo Championships, the participant should be between the ages 14–17 and hold the Kukkiwon Poom/Dan certificate in the year the championship was held.
4. The participant shall wear a Taekwondo *dobok* (uniform) and protectors recognized by the World Taekwondo Federation.
5. The participant shall wear a trunk protector, head protector, groin guard, and forearm and shin guards inside the Taekwondo uniform. Women shall wear a women's breast guard and a women's groin guard inside the uniform.
6. The use or administration of drugs or chemical substances described in the International Olympic Committee doping by-laws is prohibited.
7. The World Taekwondo Federation may carry out any medical testing deemed necessary to ascertain if a contestant has committed a breach of the drug rule. Any winner who refuses to undergo this testing or who proves to have committed such a breach shall be removed from the final standings, and the record shall be transferred to the contestant next in line in the competition standing.
8. The organizing committee shall be liable for arrangements to carry out medical testing.

PROTECTIVE GEAR

Before engaging in a supervised sparring, a student must wear the following protective gear:

Head guard

Mouth guard

Chest protector

Forearm protector

Groin protector

Shin and instep protector

Head guard

Mouth guard

Chest protector

Forearm protector

Groin protector

Shin and instep protector

PROHIBITED ACTS IN COMPETITION

The following prohibited acts *(Kyong-go)* will result in a warning with a ½-point deduction:

1. Touching Acts
   a. Grabbing the opponent.
   b. Holding the opponent.
   c. Pushing the opponent.
   d. Touching the opponent with the trunk.
2. Negative Acts
   a. Intentionally crossing the alert line.
   b. Evading by turning the back to the opponent.
   c. Intentionally falling down.
   d. Pretending injury.
3. Attacking Acts
   a. Butting or attacking with the knee.
   b. Intentionally attacking the groin.
   c. Intentionally stamping or kicking any part of the leg or foot.
   d. Hitting the opponent's face with hands or fist.
4. Undesirable Acts
   a. Gesturing to indicate scoring or deduction on the part of the contestant or the coach.
   b. Uttering undesirable remarks or any misconduct on the part of the contestant or coach.
   c. Leaving the designated mark on the part of the coach during the match.

The following prohibited acts *(Gam-Jeom)* will result in a penalty with a 1-point deduction:

1. Touching acts
   a. Throwing the opponent.
   b. Intentionally throwing down the opponent by grappling the opponent's attacking foot in the air with the arm.
2. Negative Acts
   a. Crossing the boundary line.
   b. Intentionally interfering with the progress of the match.
3. Attacking Acts
   a. Attacking the fallen opponent.
   b. Intentionally attacking the back and the back of the head.
   c. Attacking the opponent's face severely with the hand.
4. Undesirable Acts
   a. Violent or extreme remarks or behavior on the part of the contestant or the coach.
5. When a contestant refuses to comply with the competition rules or the referee's order intentionally, the referee may declare the contestant the loser by penalty.
6. When the contestant receives –3 points, the referee shall declare the contestant the loser by penalties.
7. *Kyong-go* and *Gam-jeom* shall be counted in the total score of the three rounds.

TERMINOLOGY

FOR THE BEGINNING OF CLASS

To the flags, bow!   *Kuk ki ae dae ha yo, Kyung Rea*
To the master, bow!   *Sabum nim Kae, Kyung Rea*

CARDINAL NUMBERS

1	*ha na*
2	*tul*
3	*set*
4	*net*
5	*taseot*
6	*yoseot*
7	*ilkop*
8	*yodolb*
9	*ahop*
10	*yul*
20	*semul*
21	*semul hana*
30	*sarun*
31	*sarun hana*

COMMANDS

Attention	*Chareyut*
Ready	*Joonbe*
Begin	*Si jak*
Break	*Kal yo*
Stop	*Gue mahn*
Continue	*Kea sok*
Return	*Ba ro*

GENERAL

Grand master	*Kwan jang nim*
Master	*Sabum nim*
Instructor	*Kyo sah nim*
School	*Dojang*
Uniform	*Dobok*
Grade	*Kub*
Degree	*Dan*
Flag	*Kuk ki*
Yell	*Ki hap*
Form (pattern)	*Poomse*
Black belt holder	*Yu dan ja*
Senior	*Sun bae nim*
Junior	*Who bae*
Thank you	*Kam sahab ne da*
You're welcome	*Choon mahn ae yo*

FOR THE CLOSING OF CLASS

To the flag, bow!	*kuk ki ae dae ha yo, Kyung Rea*
To the master, bow!	*Sabum nim Kea, Kyung Rea*
Taekwondo	*Tae Kwon Do*
Thank you, sir!	*Kam sahab ne da, sabum nim*
Practice is finished	*Un dong gutt*

BLOCKS

X block	*Yeot pero maggi*
High block	*Eolgul maggi*
Middle block	*Momtong maggi*
Low block	*Ahre maggi*
Knife-hand block	*Son-nal maggi*
Spreading block	*Hecho maggi*

KICKS

Front kick	*Ahp cha-gi*
Side kick	*Yop cha-gi*
Round kick	*Dolryo cha-gi*
Back kick	*Dwi cha-gi*
Hook kick	*Guligi cha-gi*
Crescent kick	*Bandul cha-gi*
Jumping kick	*Twi o-cha-gi*

MOVEMENTS

Block	*Maggi*
Strike	*Chi-gi*
Kick	*Cha-gi*
Sparring	*Kyorugi*
Holding	*Jupgi*
Thrusting	*Jirugi*
Jumping	*Twi*
Spreading	*Hecho*
Gathering	*Modoo*
Offense	*Gong-kyok*
Self-defense	*Hosinsool*

STANCES

Attention stance	*Cha-ryot sogi*
Ready stance	*Pyong-hi sogi*
Horse stance	*Juchoom sogi*
Forward stance	*Ahp-gubi sogi*
Back stance	*Dwi-gibi sogi*
Twisted stance	*Koa sigi*
Walking stance	*Ahp sogi*
Tiger stance	*Bum sogi*

About the Authors

Grand Master Soon Man Lee was born in Seoul, South Korea, and began studying Taekwondo at the age of 7. He is an International Master Instructor, International Referee, and a certified 8th degree black belt from Kukkiwon, the World Taekwondo Federation's headquarters. He has published articles in the United States Taekwondo Union's USTU Taekwondo Journal. Master Lee is known for his wisdom, honesty, great sense of justice, and his willingness to help anyone in need.

At the age of 23, Master Lee became a master instructor training students professionally. He served 3 years with the South Korean Marine Corps. He coached on the high school and college levels. He emigrated to the United States in 1982 and taught at Cabot College in California in 1983. The following year, he was a Northern California Taekwondo Team coach.

In 1985, Master Lee moved to Florida to open his first Taekwondo school in the U.S.

He relocated to Virginia Beach, Virginia, in 1989 and opened the U.S. Taekwondo Center, where he is currently teaching. In 1991, he attended the 10th World Taekwondo Championships in Athens, Greece, as the U.S. Team Manager. In 1992, he was the U.S. Team Coach in the first International Taekwondo Games in Moscow. He was the U.S. Team's head coach at the 1992 Pan American Taekwondo Championships in Colorado Springs, Colorado. He trained the U.S. Team in 1993 in the 11th World Taekwondo Championships in New York City's Madison Square Garden. Between 1992 and 1994, he served as president of the Virginia State Taekwondo Association. Master Lee was the head coach of the U.S. Team in the 1994 World Cup Taekwondo Championship, held in the Cayman Islands, British West Indies.

In 1995, Master Lee served as head coach of the U.S. Team at four major events. In May, he took the team to the Olympic Taekwondo

Festival in Rome, Italy. In July, he went with the U.S. Team to the Olympic Festival in Colorado Springs, Colorado. In September, he took the team to the Japan Open '95 Taekwondo Championship in Osaka, Japan, and in November, he took the team to the 1995 12th World Taekwondo Championship in Manila, Philippines. In September of 1996, he took the team to the Japan Open '96 Taekwondo Championship and in March to the World Cup Championship in Brazil. In March of 1997, he took the team to the World Cup in Egypt, where the team captured third place.

Grand Master Lee's wisdom, integrity, and honesty have made him a man of honor among his colleagues. At the U.S. Taekwondo Center, he is loved by parents, children, and adult students. Master Lee is highly respected for his loyalty, dedication, achievements, teaching, and, most of all, humility.

Gaetane Ricke holds a 4th degree black belt in Taekwondo certified by Kukkiwon, the World Taekwondo Federation's headquarters in Korea. Born in Canada, Ms. Ricke earned her bachelor's degree in business administration from Centenary College in New Jersey. She began to practice Taekwondo in 1989 and became deeply interested in the art. She is an instructor and certified referee in the United States Taekwondo Union. She currently works with Grand Master Soon Man Lee as Director of the U.S. Taekwondo Center in Virginia Beach, Virginia.

Index